THE BEST

ABOUT **HABITS** FOR

EXCELLENCE

How To Make Excellence A Habit
and Become Successful

Jonathan Deckard

Summary

Introduction:

Many people question how they can be highly successful, not realizing that they have what they need to do the positive they want. Because of their habits, productive people are where they are today. Habits dictate 95% of the attitude of a person.

What you are today, and what you can ever achieve, is decided by the value of the habits you form.

You, too, can be productive and lead a happy life by developing healthy habits and adopting a positive habit.

These Positive Habits Are Healthy Predictors of Greatness for thousands of years, great thinkers and philosophers have been researching success in human life. I have been researching the subject personally for over five years. What I have learned is that strong habits have been built by the very best people.

I've established important habits & practices you need to build if you want to do whatever you can to your maximum.

The practice of calm reflection in our busy western societies is almost a forgotten custom. Our daily routine is filled with noise and business. As we hurry from appointment to appointment, quiet corners, time and places of contemplation are lost or missed.

Meditate, contemplate, or just be in the present. New ideas and creativity will flood in when you create quiet space.

"In all, there's a crack, that's how the light gets in," –Leonard Cohen. There is no need to practice the art of mindlessness. Too much thought is going to tire you. It's a dangerous place to be concerned about the past or nervous about the future.

How are you going there? The past has disappeared, and the future has not existed. You've just got "Then."

The ghosts of the past still haunt us. The memories are there.

Create room for that company to crack. Take the 'Now' Build an inspiration sliver of time to reach your consciousness.

Good habits & healthy habits are one of the best ways of rising. Set a task weight loss, exercise, and compete first with an interested friend to see who is achieving the goal.

That is Blind spots apply medically to places that our eyes are unable to see. In terms of personal growth, blind spots are things we don't know about ourselves. Learning our blind spots will help us discover our enhancement areas.

One of the activities I use to find out about my blind spots is to recognize all the things/events/ people that cause me in a day.

It is always interesting to do exercise. I'm discovering new things about myself, even though I may think I already know my own blind spots. Well, I have explained the habits & practices in detail in this e-book, which can lead you toward success.

Chapter 1: What is meant by success?

Goal-Oriented

To become goal-oriented is not an easy task. You need to be a consistent setter of goals and devote yourself to working every day of your life with clear, written goals, creating regular habits. All highly productive individuals are goal-oriented intensively. People who know what exactly they want, they've written it down, they've written plans to achieve it, and as a daily routine, they update and work on their plans.

Results Driven

Results are guided by the second pattern of highly successful people. There are two procedures that make up this.

The first is the method of learning continues to make you better at what you are doing.

The second practice is the control of time. This is what means setting very clear priorities on what you are doing and then focusing on the most interesting use of your time with one mind. All the people who are really good are highly result-oriented.

Action-Oriented

It is the most critical practice for us to achieve success. It's the desire to get the job done quickly. This is the ability to develop and sustain a sense of urgency as well as a propensity towards practice. A quick pace is a key to your performance in everything you do.

To reach your most important goals, you need to conquer procrastination, put aside your worries, and release 100 percent. In themselves, the combination of goal orientation, outcome orientation, and action orientation will virtually ensure great success.

I strongly recommend that you learn to use smart goals to list goals you can measure and track.

People Oriented

This is where interactions are put at the core of your life. It is your choice to practice patience, kindness, compassion, and understanding behaviors within yourself. Practically all of your life's satisfaction comes from your ability to get along well with others.

The good news is that you agree to become a better person in your relationships with others.

The only way you can develop any habit, as Aristotle said, is to practice it on a regular basis. The more in your relationships with others, you practice being a genuinely outstanding person, the more you internalize those attributes and become that person.

Health Conscious

It means you have to watch your diet fastidiously and eat the right food in the right amounts at all times. You have to exercise regularly, using the body's muscles and joints to keep it limber and fit. And finally, you must have proper rest and leisure habits that will help you to live your years in a safe state in combination with diet and exercise.

Note, the most important thing you have in your wellbeing, and it is entirely subject to the habits you create in your way of living.

Focusing on being more friendly with the men in your life is a perfect way to encourage a healthy attitude of thinking.

Be Honest

Ultimately, more important than nearly all else is the character you create as you go through life.

Honesty means that with everything you do, you obey the "principle of truth." For yourself and the world around you. For yourself, you set very clear values, and you organize yourself around your values. You develop your vision and then live your life in accordance with your highest ideals. For anyone or anything, you will never compromise your integrity or peace of mind.

This honesty attitude is critical to your enjoyment of all the other good habits you develop.

Self-Disciplined

Self-discipline is the habit and the one practice which ensures all the others.

The most important single attribute you can build as an individual is your ability to discipline yourself, to master yourself, to control yourself. The habit of self-discipline in any field of life goes hand in hand with success.

It is possible to develop each of these habits, goal-oriented, results-driven, action-oriented, people-oriented, health-conscious, honest, and self-disciplined. Regardless of your habits, you are where you are and who you are today. Your habits have developed, often by accident, since you were a child.

Just from today, you can take complete control over the shaping of your behavior and personality. All that happens to you in the future, by making the decision to find the definition of habits right now that will lead you to great success.

And you'll enjoy having success together if you develop the same good habits that other successful people have. Your future is going to be unlimited.

The creation habits

There's a busy life. We are in the office so lost in our jobs. The day is spent building somebody else's company. It's an exchange of qualities. And we are gaining skills and experience along the way.

But one thing is to build for others. But if that's where it starts and ends, then you're giving other people your best job. Make it for you, and take the time to create it.

Begin the development of your day. Then the day is a success already. Life's long-term success and generating a legacy is just a superset of that daily commitment.

But some of us are the owls of the moon. So, whatever your choice, block the barriers from distractions and procrastination for the time you need to create and protect it diligently. Make it a habit of creating a result.

Commit to the habit of exercise

I'm too busy, and I don't have time to work out. Have you ever heard the internal noise before?

But the truth is we are human beings interconnected. The brain is located in the physical body. Mental health is interwoven with physical health.

Or it may be put on the back burner in busy family life, working, commuting, and socializing. This is fine for short bursts, but it is important to practice 3-5 days a week. It's hard to enjoy your hard-earned millions if you're dead from a heart attack.

As part of their regime, most of the top performers have exercise. The trick fits it into a frequently busy schedule.

It's simply the two top tips that worked for me. Habitual exercise has to be comfortable and pleasant. It's easier to avoid and procrastinate if they don't tick those boxes. It's been running for me for decades, but it's road cycling today.

At 30 you may not accept the truism "If you don't use it you lose it," but at 50 you will realize the clear reality.

The habit of continuous learning

Committing to a continuous education life's habit is one of the strongest habits you can follow. A college or university degree is not the end of your learning, but a step towards awareness and wisdom.

"You mostly learn best by reading a lot and writing a lot in your daily routine, and those you teach yourself are the most valuable lessons of all. This applies to any kind of mastery. It might be watching a TED talk or listening to a podcast, not just reading.it. We all have different learning methods. Make your daily routine part of continuous learning.

The time block habit

They're all over the place. Mobile phones, app warnings, and even massive freeway TV screens. No wonder the rate of accidents is not going down. But interruptions are more insidious.

And they do not come with a health warning, and they've slipped into our corporate, company, and daily habits. It's those horrific diversions of science.

It's a mistake for many of us to always check your emails. There's another, even worse, more dangerous communication technology.

More than 1 billion people now use the "Messenger" of Face book. The version of Skype is called "Instant Messenger." And for all of our social networks, many of us have alerts running on our smartphones. I don't know about you, but it's not the right place to be and a time drain to be at the beck and call for other people's priorities.

Well-used instant messaging is a great tool, but it's always wrong. Time blocking is a daily habit and strategy worth cultivating to get real work done and generate something of consequence. Interrupt out regular time for ventures and development that make a difference The Dwight Eisenhower efficiency advice is worth considering.

"What is critical is rarely urgent, and it is rarely important what is urgent." Routine trends of progress the truth that we know?

Concentrate if we are to create meaningful and purposeful long-term success. And I promise you this. That is going to make you happy.

Block time for significant projects and deep work each day that will create real progress over time. To be successful and efficient, however, turning off your phone, messaging, and social media alerts are vital tactics. Make time to block your routine every day.

Create a community and relationship habit

"Good relationships make us healthier and happier." That's what it is.

It's not difficult. But we're still chasing money, fame, and things. Nourishing your friends and family relationships is something we need to appreciate more and make a habit.

My good friend has a serious routine focused on this topic. Some people might call it obsessive. For their birthday, he directly calls 1,800 people a year. It's his grandfather's influenced habit. He wanted people to know how special they are.

So maybe we're not all inspired to call almost 2,000 people a year to say happy birthday, but you're getting the message. So, cultivate your relationships and continue to build a community, and there will be happiness.

The habit of persistence

A word at the time and eventually, the answer is rejected. But it's all that it is. It looks too simply to be true, but if you want to one stone at a time, imagine China's Great Wall. That's the whole thing one stone in a row.

The process of constantly working and strapping yourself in and doing the work will create a body of work that will define you. It's something worth pursuing that sense of achievement.

Develop the organized habit

When your life is out of control, and everything is a mess, so it's hard to survive when it's not a pure and lucky accident. Yet that's not so much the case.

Here's the kind of stuff which happens when you're coordinated and disciplined. Don't file in time your tax return further fees and maybe a fine. Forget to pay for registering your car. More fines and a permit can be lost.

Should you not arrange and file your office processes? You're going to spend double the time doing things. Coordinated can be seen as dull for those of us tactical imaginative types that are fluffy.

Hire an accountant or personal assistant, or even a cleaner if you just hate doing it. Hire someone who has the process and attention to the DNA gene in detail (even part-time).

Life's habit of being messy can turn into a slow spiral into disaster. It's going to be a daily confrontation for some of us.

A final thought Hoping for that prescription or template for success, you may have shown up here. The truth? There's no one here. Just a couple of hints and suggestions I found on the journey.

"If you consider carefully what you're going to say about your funeral. Your concept of success will be found there".

11

Chapter 2: Set Priorities for the Successful Life

2.1 The ABCDE method

Set Goals the ABCDE method is a powerful technique for setting priorities that can be used every day. This method is so simple and effective that it can make you one of the field's most efficient and effective people. The ABCDE chart is a drug to - do guide while learning how to prioritize.

This technique's power lies in its simplicity because it is so action-oriented.

Here's how it works: begin with a list of all you've got to do for the day to come. Think about the journal. Begin the ABCDE method once you have a list of all the tasks you need to complete.

"A" item is the much important object of An A is described as something very important. That's something you have to do.

It is a job in which when you fail to do it, this can have significant consequences. Consequences such as not visiting a trick client or not completing a document that she wants for an upcoming board meeting for the supervisor.

These are life's frogs.

When you have better than one "A" task, prioritize these tasks in front of every item at writing A-1, A-2, A-3, and so on. The A-1 job is your greatest, most ugly frog of all.

"B" items Just Have Minor Impacts A B item is defined as a task you will perform. So, it has just moderate effects.

These are your job life's tadpoles. This means that if you don't perform it, someone might be upset or uncomfortable, so it doesn't matter as much as an A task. This would be a B task to return an unimportant telephone message or to check your email.

The rule is that if there is an A task left undone, you cannot do a B task. Once there is a big frog sitting there waiting to be eaten, you should not be bothered by a tadpole.

"C" Tasks Have No Consequences abcde-list-sidebar-banner A C task is something that would be nice to do but for which, whether you do it or not, there are no consequences at all.

C tasks include calling a friend, having coffee or lunch with a coworker, or completing some business during focusing hours. Such operation has no effect whatsoever on the working life.

As a rule, if there are B or A tasks left unfinished, you can never complete a C task.

"D" something that you surely can delegate to someone else for the Delegate A D event.

The rule is that you should delegate to other people as much as you can. This should allow you more time to engage in your activities. The full course of your career is largely determined by your tasks and their completion.

"E" An E event to remove is something you should completely eliminate.

After all, if you rest doing stuff that you no longer need to do, you can only keep your time under control.

The key to making it ABCDE process work is to motivate yourself now to begin your "A-1" task immediately. Hang there until it's finished. Use your willpower to do this one job, the most important task you would be able to do. Eat a whole frog, and don't stop until. it's all over.

Invest your time on productive tasks. The springboard to higher rates of accomplishment is your ability to think about and evaluate your worklist to assess your "A-1" task. It also results in increased self-esteem, self-respect, and personal pride.

When you develop the habit of working on your "A-1," you're going to start doing more than anyone around you.

Make a rule to never do something on your agenda that isn't. If a new task or task comes up, write it down on your list before you start working on it and set a goal for it.

You will easily lose control of your day if you react and respond to the nonstop demands on your time. We end up spending most of your precious time and energy low- or no-value activities.

Check the list you are currently working on and put an A, B, C, D, or E next to each task or activity. Pick your work or project A-1 and immediately start on it. Motivate yourself to do nothing else until you have completed this one job. It will become one of the best tools you can use to control your time.

Practice this ABCDE method every day and for the next month on each work or project list before you start work. At that time, the habit of setting and working on your highest priority tasks will have been developed. The future is going to be safe!

2.2 Manage stress through Sports and physical activity.

"I take time to in three ways. The first is through intense adrenaline sports, like downhill cycling or competitive skiing, which require concentration and ability to be ready for unforeseen obstacles, or to regulate [high] speeds in skiing, acting as both safe distractions and physical training.

Plan the minutes of your day.

"I'm pretty obsessed with my schedule. Every second of the day is accounted for. To make sure that I am spending my precious time on things that drive progress. I do not want to get sucked into replying to emails or getting distracted. I'm not just planning meetings, but working on projects or tasks, clearing up emails, dreaming, brainstorming, and planning for the week ahead.

2.3 Start the day with meditations.

"Daily morning, I wake up with a cup of tea and then mediate in the quietness of my living room for 10 minutes. I like to begin my day with purpose, and meditation helps me focus my mind on what I want to achieve in my company, personal life, health, and relationships. The mind is a very powerful weapon, and when you concentrate your energy on a small set of goals, amazing things start to happen.

Become a reader.

I am a good reader of mysteries and history. I had started when I was a child. Now I have grown to love historical bios and today's political essay. It's a great escape to jump through novels into a new or unfamiliar environment, which has broadened my perspective and the genuine interest in specific historical periods or the political context of today.

2.4 Actively remove distractions.

One of today's world's greatest challenges is to separate yourself from all the noise of life. I use noise-canceling headphones to eliminate interference and do not listen to any popular songs. I consider my attention growing exponentially with fewer distractions, and I'm much more successful.

Try to spend time alone

"I always try to find time alone in the morning, whether it is walking the dog or eating breakfast to set my priorities clearly, so I know what I want to accomplish each of my days. I make sure to mark not only for my personal priorities, but also priorities for my team and concern persons, so I can be sure both works get done one the time. Once I get into my office, my day becomes about how can I take any kind of obstacles out of the way for my team members, so they can execute and do their work at the highest levels on their priorities. I would like to call this working on the business instead of the business. Empowering your employees to take their best work, has always been the key to my success and achievements, as well as being the hallmark of a world-class organization.

Read something for pleasure

"I especially take our time in the morning to eat balanced breakfast and read something good that is not related t to work to give it my best each day. That helps me relax my mind. I'm fired up and ready to go by the time I leave for work.

2.5 Maximize your time by using commutes

"I try to maximize my time by planning and thinking during my commute. I jog or bike to work most days a week to allow my mind time to decompress and think about business issues. Research has demonstrated that exercise enhances memory and learning, and I found it helps my creativity. Often thoughts that normally come to me during my trip are the basis for the company's guidance within the next week or month."

Never leave any emails unread.

My inbox has null or close to zero emails, and for years it's been like that. My rules are: First, if I receive an email, I will respond to it as soon as possible if I think my response is needed. Secondly, if I have to think about it, I'm going to do it mostly in 24 hours or accept it if it takes longer. Third, I'm not going to respond to them if they don't follow the first or second rule. Third, I'm going to put a rule to auto-delete them for topics that I'm not involved in so that I don't waste my time. It helps me stay successful and be on top of things.

2.6 Smile and talk to strangers.

"As I grew up, it was normal behavior to look at someone in the eye and smile at them as they walked up to you on the sidewalk. I found myself conforming, and then learned that just saying 'Good morning' to someone in the elevator or having a short chat with my Uber driver would give me the opportunity to talk.

Gets the ball rolling earlier?

Starting my day early with a productivity-based morning routine helps set the day's tone. It looks like a typical morning for me. I'm going to answer any outstanding messages over coffee, network a little by the posting on LinkedIn, or read the news and catch up on current events, review my calendar and send any requests or questions that came up overnight in my mind.

Avoid meetings and don't allow briefings.

"I limit the number of meetings I am involved in and do not allow briefings where the meeting is dominated by presenting recaps, incomplete information, or information that everyone already knows. Send an update in advance so that the meeting can be debated and challenging, not staring at PowerPoints.

Proactively manage decision fatigue.

"Humans can be amazingly bad at managing and recognizing the impact of decision-making fatigue (the tendency to make worse choices after prolonged decision-making sessions when they are cognitively exhausted) In order to combat this phenomenon, I move my highest priority meetings to mid-morning when I am most alerted and try to limits the number of decisions that I make after lunch.

Keep up on what is going on outside of yourself

"My goal is to build an external perspective every day. I do this in many different ways. I spend 30 to 45 minutes, keeping up on what's going on outside my own environment. When you concentrate only on what's impacting your business or industry, you might skip the forest of the trees.

Eat dinner as a family every night

"I make sure that dinner time with my family is a ritual that is protected and prioritized. We all sit down together every evening and connect face-to-face (electronics are banned from the table) No matter what's going on at work, I commit to dinner at home, and I'm 100% present to catch up with my family.

Leave your phone at night, especially.

My brain needs a break from vibration and noise of my mobile in an ever-connected world: a new message to respond to, a flame to put out, or an idea to ponder. To counter it, when I go to sleep, I never bring my phone into my bedroom to make sure I physically disconnect every day. Life is more than just a task.

Chapter 3: Self-improvement

3.1 Self-improvement phase1

Read a book every day.

Books are condensed information sources. The more books you're reading, the more wisdom you're exposed to.

What are some books to enrich yourself, you can start reading? Some books that I have read and found helpful are Think and Grow Rich, Who Moved My Cheese, Habits, Getting Rich Science and Living the 80/20 Way.

You will fill your brain with more and more knowledge as you read a book every day. Do you know the best way to store all this information and knowledge? This Virtual Brain is what you need.

Learn a new language.

English is my main language. I have been taking language courses in recent years, such as Japanese and Bahasa Indonesian, out of curiosity.

I learned that learning a language is a whole new skill, and getting to know a new language and culture is a totally open-minded experience.

Pick up a new hobby.

Fencing, golf, rock climbing, soccer, canoeing, or ice skating are examples.

It can also be a fun sport for your new hobby — for example, pottery, Italian cooking, dancing, web design, wine appreciation, etc.

Learning something new allows you to stretch yourself, physically, mentally, or psychologically, in different aspects.

Take up a new course.

Courses are a perfect way to acquire new skills and knowledge.

It doesn't have to be long- course seminars or workshops are also serving their purpose.

I went to a few workshops, and they helped me gain new insights that I hadn't thought about before.

Create an inspirational room.

Your setting provides you with the atmosphere and voice. You're going to be inspired every day if you're living in an inspiring setting.

I haven't really liked my space in the past because I felt it was messy and slow. The final outcome? A house in which I completely enjoy being and encourage me every day to be at my best.

Overcome your fears.

We're all afraid. Fear of uncertainty, fear of speaking to the society, fear of risk. All our worries trap us in the same position and keep us from through.

Recognize that the areas where you can grow reflect your worries. I always see fears as the creation compass.

If I'm afraid of something, it's something I still have to deal with, and confronting it helps me grow.

Level up your skills.

If you have previously played video games, particularly RPGs, you will be familiar with the concept of leveling up – gaining experience so that you can be better and stronger.

I am constantly upgrading my writing skills as a writer. As a speaker, I continually upgrade my ability to engage with the public.

Wake up early.

I believe it's because you're already set to continue the momentum and live the day proactively when you wake up early.

Have a weekly exercise routine

A better starting point for you to be in better physical shape. At least three days a week, at least 30 minutes every day, I actually make it a point to jog.

Start your life handbook

A manual of life is a concept which I started three years ago.

It's essentially a book that contains the essential elements of how you can live your life to the fullest, such as your meaning, principles, and goals, kind of like your life's guide.

Since 2007, I began my life manual, and it has been a key enabler in my development.

Write a letter to your future self

Five years from now, what do you see yourself? Are you going to be the same? The other way around? Which sort of person wants to be?

Write a letter or note to your future self for the future – it will be a good start for one year from now – and seal it.

Make a date for opening it one year from now on your calendar. Then practice becoming the person you want that letter to be opened.

3.2 Self-improvement phase 2

Get out of your comfort zone

From hard work and sweat, real growth arrives. It doesn't allow us to grow too relaxed, and it makes us stagnate.

What's your place of comfort? Were you staying for the most part? When you go out with other people, do you keep your own space? Shake up your routine. Do something other than that.

By adapting yourself to a new context, because you learn to act in new circumstances, you are actually developing.

Ask for feedback

We'll always have blind spots as much as we try to improve. Requesting reviews give us additional insight.

Most people to target will be family, relatives, bosses, bosses, or even acquaintances, as they will have no inherent bias and will be able to give impartial feedback.

Stay focused on to-do lists.

I begin my day with a list of tasks that I want to complete, which helps me stay focused. The days when I don't do this, in comparison, end up being highly unproductive, for example, writing a guest post at Lifehack. E-Book writing is part of my to-do list for today, and that's why I'm writing this now! I use Free Sticky Notes to control my to-do lists as my work requires me to use my computer all the time. It's really easy to use, and its freeware, so I recommend you to try it out.

Set Big Hairy Audacious Goals (BHAGs).

I'm a big fan of the BHAG system. BHAGs push you beyond your normal ability as they're wide and daring – you wouldn't even think of trying them. What are BHAGs that you can embark on, which you will feel on top of the world when you complete them? Set them up and begin to work on them and learn how to make highly successful use of SMART goals in life.

Acknowledge your flaws

That is. Everyone has shortcomings. What is most important is that they are heard, acknowledged, and discussed. What do you think your shortcomings are? What are the shortcomings that you can work on now? How are you going to tackle them?

Get into action

Action is the best way to improve. What was the intention of you to do? How can you take immediate action on it? Waiting has nothing to do with it. Taking action will send you immediate results from which to learn.

Learn from people who inspire you

Think of people that you respect. Individuals that inspire you. Such people also represent some of the attributes you want to have for yourself. What are the attributes you want for yourself in them? How can these values be acquired?

Quit a bad habit.

Will you break some bad habits? Overcoming? Are you not exercising? Is it too late? Did you slouch? Are you biting the nail? Do you smoke?

Here's some great advice on hacking your habit loop from Lifehack's CEO to break bad habits and build good ones and how to break a habit and hack the habit loop.

Cultivate a new habit

Some good new cultivation habits include reading books, early morning, exercising, reading a new article about personal development a day, and meditation. Can you cultivate any other new habit to improve yourself?

3.3 Self-improvement phase3

Avoid negative people

"You are the average of the four to five people with whom you spend most of your time."

Wherever we go, negative people are bound to be there. If you feel they drag you down, don't spend too much of your time around them.

Learn to deal with difficult people

There are times when you can't avoid hard people like at your office, or when the individual is part of your inner touch circle.

Learn how to handle them. Such skills towards managing people will go a long way in the future, working with people how to deal with people who are negative.

Learn from your friends

Everyone has amazing qualities. It's up to how we're going to tap them. They're going to have things you do learn about with all the people that surround you.

Try to think right now of a good friend. Only think of one value that you want to follow. How can you learn from them and make your own use of this skill? If you need to, talk to them. They will surely be more than happy to help!

Start a journal

Journaling is a great way to become more aware of yourself. It's a process of self-reflection.

You gain more insight about yourself as you write, explain your thinking process, and read what you wrote from the perspective of a second person.

It can be a personal journal or an online blog. I also use my personal development site as a private journal, and through the past year of writing and reading, I've learned a lot about myself.

Start a blog about personal development

That is, you need to walk the talk first to help others learn. There are expectations that you have to uphold, both from yourself and from others.

I'm running the Personal Excellence Blog, where I share my personal journey and insights into living a better life. Readers look to my articles in order to improve themselves, which makes it clear to myself. I need to keep improving for myself, especially, and for the people I reach out to.

Reduce the time you spend on chats.

I found that in a lot of wasted time, chat programs were available by default. This time can be spent on other things even better.

The days I'm not chatting, I'm doing a lot more. In chat programs, I typically disable the auto-start option, so launch it when I want to chat and have the energy for it.

Learn chess (or any strategy game).

I find that chess is a great game to learn the strategy and fine-tune the brainpower. Not only are you having fun, but your analytical skills can also be practiced.

From other board games or computer games like Othello, Chinese Chess, Warcraft, and so on, you can also learn strategy.

Stop watching TV

I haven't watched television for almost four years, and it was a very liberating experience I found that most of the mainstream television programs and commercials are usually of a lower consciousness and not very strong.

In return, the time that I freed myself from not watching TV is now being used constructively for other reasons, such as interacting with close friends, doing work that I enjoy, exercising, etc.

Start a 30-day challenge

To do this, set a goal and give yourself 30 days. Your goal may be to stick to a new habit or something you've always wanted to do but didn't.

It's just 30 days to prepare, plan, take action, update, and nail the target.

Meditate

Meditation helps calm you down and make you more conscious. I also realized that I need less sleep during the nights I meditate (before I sleep). The process of clearing up the clutter is very liberating.

3.4 Self-improvement phase4

Join Toastmasters (Learn public speaking).

Ironically, the one fear in the world is public speaking, with 2 being death.

After I began speaking in public as a speaker/trainer for personal development, I have learned a lot about it. To communicate better, present me, and engage people. Toastmasters is a public-speaking international organization that trains people.

Befriend top people in their fields

These people have achieved their success as they have the right personalities, sets of skills, and know-how. How better to learn from and do that from the people who were there? Gain from them fresh perspectives on how you can improve yourself to produce the same results.

Let go of the past

Which is there any bitterness or unhappiness which you get taken on from the past? If so, the time has come to let go of it.

Holding on to them makes it difficult for you to move on and become a better person. Forgive yourself, break free from the past, and move on.

I have moved on from a 5-year-old childhood heartbreak just recently. The result was empowering and powerful, and I was never happier.

Start a business venture

Are you interested in anything? Why not make it a project and make money while at the same time learning?

Starting a new company involves mastering the skills of business management, cultivating business acumen, and getting a competitive edge.

The process of starting and improving my company in personal growth has provided me many skills, such as self-discipline, leadership, organization, and management.

Show kindness to people around you

That's right. You can't be too compassionate to anybody. In reality, most of us don't express the men around us enough kindness.

Being kind allows one to grow other attributes like compassion, patience, and love.

After reading this book today, when you return to your day, begin to exude more kindness to the people around you and see that they respond.

Remember how you feel like being kind to others, not just that. Chances are, you're going to look better than you are.

Reach out to those people who hate you most

You're going to get haters if you're ever fighting for something. Hating the people who hate us is simple. Loving them back is a number more challenging.

It takes magnanimity and an open heart to be able to forgive, let go, and show love to these people.

Is there anyone in your life who dislikes or hates you? If so, get in touch with them.

Look for a settlement and have past cases closed. Even though they refuse to reciprocate, they still love them. It's much more rewarding than hating them again.

Take a break

Did you build too hard? It is also about self-improvement to recognize our need to take a break to walk the longer mile ahead. You can't drive a car if it doesn't have gasoline.

It is important to plan downtime on your own. Take yourself some time off every week. Relax, rejuvenate, and fight for what's in front of you.

Read at least 1 or 2 personal-development articles daily

Some readers make it a point to read every day at least one personal development article that I think is an excellent habit.

There are a lot of great personal development blogs out there, some of which can be reviewed here.

Commit to your personal growth

I can write books on the list with ten ways, 25 ways, 42 ways, or even 1,000 ways of improving habits, but if you don't want to contribute to your personal growth, it doesn't matter what I write.

There's nothing going to get through. We are responsible, not someone else, for our personal growth, not your mother, not your father, not your friend, not me or Lifehack.

Decide to commit to your personal development and welcome yourself on a life-long growth and transformation journey. Begin your development with a few of the above measures and work on them. There may be no immediate results, but I guarantee

Chapter 4: Challenge Your Self

4.1 (30-day) challenge

You should initiate developing healthy behaviors today when you want to lead a happier life. The 30-day challenge is one way to ensure these healthy habits are permanently part of your system. We 30-day challenge ideas to you today to boost your career, private life, health, finances, relationships, and much the planet. You will choose the ones that are many important to you. How does the Challenge 30-Day work?

It is challenging to start a new habit. It's even more difficult to crack a bad one.

We also seek to remove our bad habits. Life generally gets in the way, sadly. In a couple of days, we may be fine, but something still stops us from forming a lifelong habit.

And why often do we fail?

The problem is that terrifying term – permanent.

It's hard to persuade yourself, deep in our subconscious, that you have to do it forever. We don't like the idea of spending the remainder of our lives doing an unpleasant activity. The problem with it seems to be forever.

Simply put, it's challenging to get past the first few weeks of a change in habit. It is the moment once most people are succumbing to their impulses. It is easier to stick to a new routine when you pass this crucial period.

In a way, the mind is fooled by a 30-day challenge to develop a new habit. When you think it's just in a month, it's easy to do something unpleasant. And when the time is up, you're going to be close to making a positive change.

Let's say you're a smoker, for example. Many people can't break that habit because never having another cigarette can't be committed. Most people have no willingness to go like this "cold turkey."

A safer approach is to concentrate on a couple of weeks on developing a new habit. Basically, you are taking it for a "test drive." You're going to try a habit for a while and see through it works instead of committing to a permanent change.

30 Days is not a guarantee that the results you expect from a lifestyle change will be achieved. Indeed, one study claims that sticking to a new habit takes an average of 66 days.

However, thirty days is enough for you to find out if your strategy will job in the long run or if you need to change the approach.

Though the strategy works, this amount of time also gets the ball rolling, so you have the power of will to get the habit embedded in your system.

Let's explore your personal 30-day challenge with some ideas! What you'll know at Work.

4.2 (100 marvelous tips)

1-10

Wear something good to work that makes you feel like your best

Well, dressing and good grooming may improve confidence in yourself.

The downside to being in the office well-dressed is that you win attention from other men.

Apply the Pomodoro Technique in your work

The Pomodoro Strategy allows you to improve your performance and your ability to maximize your work time.

List the key tasks you need to accomplish to apply the strategy in your work. Then set a 25-minute timer and begin working on the tasks you have listed. Try to go even if distractions exist. Take a 5-minute break after 25 minutes. Then do an additional 25 minutes of continuous work.

Keep a routine daily journal

Take time to think about what happened at the office at the end of the day. This exercise helps you to convey the mixed feelings that you may have about your work or experience.

The log can also act as evidence for events that have happened in the past, which will need to be checked in the future (e.g., the date you have been promoted or the time you have had to deal with a rough client). You can also clear your mind by writing in your work journal so that you can focus on new tasks.

Avoid checking emails

Make it a point to stop reading your email as soon as you arrive at school to maintain your attention because you concentrate on the tasks you are expected to do. Alternatively, first, focus on something critical.

You should test your inbox after you've done it. This way, you stay unaware of the funny cat videos that your cousin sent you, the two-day sale they have for your favorite store, or the report that your team needs to send out within a week (important but not an emergency).

This is guaranteed to increase your productivity about the next 30 days and teach you how to come to things done properly.

Arrive 30 minutes early for work

Arriving at work a couple of minutes earlier not only increases productivity but also decreases pressure when driving. If you make this a habit of getting to work early, you will be seen by managers and co-workers as someone who is trustworthy. You show that you are able to carry a reasonable share of the workload of the day.

Too early for work, however, reduces its benefits. Ideally, arriving early in half an hour gives you peace and quiet to do a couple of things before the whole office gets busy.

Improve your skills that are relevant to your work

A technical credential helps improve your career in a variety of ways, including hiring, having a promotion, getting better pay, and taking on new responsibilities. By enrolling in a course online or through a brick-and-mortar school near your area, you can get a certification.

Day obstacle | 30-day fitness challenge thoughts | 30-day weight loss challenge ideas Getting a professional certificate helps boost your career, such as hiring, getting a promotion, or even paying more.

About personal fitness trainers, foreign language teachers, IT professionals, and web developers, some in-demand certifications today are available.

Brainstorm solutions

To improve imagination and important thinking skills, brainstorming is a good way. Identify a dilemma or challenge at work for the next 30 days. This problem might affect you personally, or it might be a problem that your team or department is currently working to solve.

Write down your proposed solutions and try to apply the solutions if you get the opportunity. In addition, if you've been brainstorming for a solution to your group's problem, share your ideas at your next meeting. Pay your colleague a compliment.

This one is tricky because you don't want to sound fake when you give a compliment to a co-worker. In addition, you don't want your colleague to believe you're behaving superior, and it's your duty to check their work's quality. Make sure you have a genuine compliment.

Always be mindful of your posture

There are many benefits to reasons the correct posture, especially while sitting down for an extended period of time. A bad posture affects your digestion (making you vulnerable to acid reflux), prevents you from properly breathing, and causes you to suffer from sore muscles.

The weight on both sides of the thighs will be fairly distributed. Test the straight and comfortable back. You ought to match your head with your collarbones.

Avoid using contractions in conversations

While contractions are helpful in conversations, their frequent use often emphasizes the negative (e.g., they can't, don't, won't). Instead of you can say I do not want to go to the beach for a company outing. I will prefer a mountain resort for the company outing site.

10-20

Refrain from using your phone during working time

Go on tech detox for the next thirty days by refraining from using tech devices while you're at work. Use it for that purpose only if you use your cellphone as an alarm clock. Stop using your mobile and other devices as you ride to and from work as an extra challenge.

During lunch break get out of your desk

Take the time to recharge by leaving your desk at lunchtime in the middle of the day. Take with you a light lunch and go for a short walk. Having lunch out will help you relinquish work-related stress and give you an energy boost to deal with the rest of the day.

Read posts with recipes that you can make in an hour or less if you need some ideas for healthy lunches.

Take a 30-day vacation from work

Would you like to have a fresher perspective on the workplace? Give yourself time by taking a month-long vacation to refresh and regroup.

It can boost your creativity and physical health by taking 30 days off from work. Use the time to get back in touch with your parents.

Make sure to let your employers know a few weeks ahead before switching to holiday mode completely.

Personal Development Challenges 14. Determine your day

Determine your priorities for the day

Use the Eisenhower matrix to disagree on what is important and urgent to get out of every single day for the next thirty days. This approach is one of the easiest ways to overcome procrastination altogether.

Use a gratitude journal

Journal in appreciation. Transform your life outlook and gain more satisfaction by writing in a journal of appreciation for what you are thankful for. To start your journey to gratitude, check here if you need some writing prompts.

Also, if you still decide on the form of a journal of gratitude to use, our 2019 analysis of the best journals of gratitude can help you make the right choice.

Organize your digital files.

You may discover several important ones that you have been hunting for weeks or even months after organizing your files. You'll also get your computer out of the clutter, making it work more efficiently.

Meditate

You should begin meditating once a day to develop a habit of mindfulness.

Improved memories, reduced anxieties, reduced cravings for cigarettes and junk food, and a strengthened immune system are some of the most beneficial you will receive when you meditate for a month.

Do something that promotes self-care.

For your physical and mental health, self-care is the most important thing you can do.

Take the time to develop a self-care routine for the next four weeks. You do not have to spend a lot to look after yourself. In reality, some of the activities require nothing from you to spend.

Create a morning routine

We believe that one of the foundations for success is a good morning routine. So why don't you develop a great morning routine like your 30DC?

Several apps are available to help you start your morning routine. Find one for you that suits you well.

Learn two new words every day

Why don't you learn some words if you want to develop a stronger vocabulary? Open the dictionary and select two words for each day randomly.

30 Day Engagement Challenge Monthly Challenges 2019 30 Day Challenge Ideas Food Practice two new words can boost your vocabulary every day.

Two new words a day, 30 days at the end of the competition is equivalent to 60 new words!

20-30

Try your hands at arts and crafts

That's right. Not only children can profit from doing arts and crafts. For adults, after a difficult day, craftsmanship can be a way to reduce stress.

It also helps us to keep the mind sharp, fosters creativity, and increases levels of self-confidence. More importantly, studies have shown that the arts and crafts on patients who use this as a creative outlet can reduce the impact of serious diseases.

Maybe it's time to consider taking that lesson of knitting.

Practice calligraphy

Calligraphy practice is one specific way of learning the arts and crafts. Calligraphy strengthens your vision and promotes mental health.

It's not just a charming talent. It's pretty useful too. Once you've mastered this, for the special occasions in your life, you won't have to pay for expensive invitation cards. You can do it yourself!

Learn a foreign language

Within 30 days, challenge yourself to grasp a foreign language's foundations. A better way to do this is through an app for language learning.

Using apps, you can quickly immerse yourself in learning the vocabulary and grammar rules of a language for 10 minutes a day until you are able to hold basic conversations in that language.

Be a mindful listener

The most important gift you can give to someone to today's mobile tech era becomes your full, undivided attention. One way to do that work is through the management of listening carefully.

Know how to be a good listener for the entire month. You will deepen your relationships with others and become better acquainted with yourself.

Discover different ways of being happy

What exactly makes you happy? Prepare a list of the things to events inside you that spark joy.

Try the best to buy or try at least one thing on your everyday agenda.

Enroll in a 30-day online course

By enrolling in a course you're really interested in, you will nurture a growth mindset. Most widely regarded colleges are offering huge open online courses these days. Some of them can be accessed through a site such as Coursera.

Make the goal to complete it when you have chosen your course. You'll be on the right path to know new skills and knowledge!

Read something for 20 minutes each day

Whether it's some pages of a book you're reading at the moment, a few magazine articles, a related blog post, or a review of other books, prepare it a point to do some reading every day for at least 20 minutes.

Make your bed upon waking up

Make your bed first in the morning if you want to begin your day with more positivity and a stronger sense of accomplishment.

You will also find that beginning other healthy daily habits is simpler once you start making your bed every morning.

Engage in random acts of kindness

As science has proved, doing random acts of kindness actually helps you to live longer. Being kind also boosts confidence in yourself and can reduce pressure and anxiety.

Go out of your comfort zone as your next 30-day challenge and do something that will help or cheer someone up (either a person you know or a stranger). Do it without thinking about rewards, rather than simply focusing on bringing happiness into someone's day.

30-40

Write thank-you note

Seek to show your gratitude if you want to encourage more positivity in your life. One more way to do this is to write thank-you notes to people who have supported you or contributed positively to your life.

Writing to one person a day is your challenge. Be clear about exactly what you are thinking that person, for example, thank you for the constant encouragement you gave me when I had a rough time starting my business. Whether you want to post the notes or not, it's up to you.

Draw or doodle

You'll enjoy drawing or doodling something for the next 30 days if you're creative. In addition, this practice has a range of beneficial health benefits.

Doodling and drawing are perfect ways of staying in the present. Doodling also helps alleviate stress and process challenging feelings as well as improve our concentration.

Finally, the daily doodle is a great way to improvise your creativity and performance.

Watch one documentary per day

Want to become more intelligent? It helps you achieve this goal by watching documentaries.

Consider watching a documentary a day a personal challenge. By introducing yourself to other cultures, lifestyles, and schools of thought, this helps expand your knowledge base.

Take time to enjoy the sunrise and sunset

Watching sunrise & sunset for the next thirty days, deepen your love for the beauty of nature. As a bonus, there are health benefits of observing the rising or setting of the sun.

Instagram 30-day challenge ideas personal challenge examples 30-day fitness plan ideas Take time to enjoy sunrise or sunset.

This can reduce anxiety symptoms, reinforce the immune system, and stabilize your mood.

Doing this as a 30DC will reduce anxiety symptoms, improve the immune system, and regulate the mood.

Dedicate one hour each day for your self

We still feel guilty of taking time off our daily duties to have some "me" time. Numerous studies have shown, however, that spending quality time with us not only has a positive impact on our personal health but also trickles the benefits into other aspects of our lives (e.g., family and career).

Carve out an hour each day as a reward for the next 30 days, which you will dedicate to yourself exclusively. We can read a book (as part of another challenge of 30 days), meditate, or just do some self-care exercises that nourish your soul.

Allow yourself to worry

One effective method to reduce anxiety and rumination is to set aside for "worry time" for 15 to 30 minutes per day. Although it seems counterproductive, research shows that spending several minutes focusing on things that make you nervous that actually reduces the duration and intensity of worrying thoughts throughout the day.

Write down all the things you're thinking about in that half-hour window. There are no big or small issues. It's reasonable to think about anything. Get all your feelings of distaste on paper, then quit when you've run out of the time.

Try to do this for the next thirty days and see the change in your attitude and outlook.

Learn how to bake

Baking is a cooking life skill subcategory. And as a bonus, you can use your ability to show your love for others if you know how to cook. You can potentially turn baking into an income-generating way as well.

Just know how to bake, you don't have to enroll in a cooking school. The Internet is a very good bakery resource. For your personal challenge for the next 30 days, you will learn everything you need to know about baking bread, cakes, cookies, and other pastries.

Use kind words with yourself

We are often guilty of negative self-talking. So, make it a continuous habit to just say kind words to yourself for the next 30 days.

Listen to your favorite music

Listen to your favorite music every day if you're looking for a way to improve your mood. Try it this a month and see how it improves your outlook.

You can also increase your productivity by listening to music you enjoy, avoid your cravings for junk food, and improve your ability to retain knowledge. Play your playlist in your car, at work, at home, and while you're working out.

Go outdoors

Did you know that physicians now recommend time to heal what their patients are doing in nature? Health problems such as chronic pain, poor eyesight, and mood disorders can all be minimized or cured when you spend time outside.

In addition, people who interact with nature on a daily basis feel more at peace and are able to cope with challenges in their lives.

30 Day challenge ideas for weight loss 30 Day workout challenges list Annual challenges Go outdoors and connect with nature, helping you feel more at ease and more concentrated on solving your life's challenges.

How about going every day this month to a nearby park during your lunch break?

Become a volunteer

Volunteering helps people in need, but it's not just the benefits to those you help. You can benefit from voluntary work.

If you volunteer, you communicate with other people in a meaningful manner. You're making friends as well. In fact, volunteering gives you a sense of mission and increases your level of happiness and well-being.

It is important to find the right place to volunteer. Research multiple organizations or ask about opportunities to volunteer in your community.

Write a quote for the day.

Reading inspirational quotes on a daily basis, you will change your life for the better. Motivational and inspiring words help to bring about your desired success and happiness.

Read it many times or write it in your journal when you have chosen a quote for the day. Reflect the meaning of the quote and how to apply the message to your life. Then use the quote all day long as a reference.

Spend a few minutes doing some coloring

Adult coloring books have several benefits. Coloring is therapeutic in the first place. It relaxes you, and the joy of childhood reminds you.

It can also act as a form of meditation, taking you to a state of mind that lets you focus on the present moment.

Watch a TED Talk video

Get a dose of inspiration every day by watching TED Talks that ignite your interest. Watch one clip a day and see how the perspective changes.

Take different photographs

You deepen your appreciation for life by taking pictures of things that spark joy. For the next 30 days, make this a regular routine, then see how the perspective has changed.

As an additional challenge, print out the pictures you took at the end of the 30 days and frame them. Hang them as reminders of how wonderful life is in your mirror.

Visit the local library

For the next 30 days, leaving your phone at home and visiting the local library is one way to get rid of social media.

Besides being the most accessible way to access books, through reading clubs, libraries offer opportunities to socialize.

Practice a party trick

30-day challenges Tumblr monthly challenges 2018 30-day video challenge list Performing a party trick can also improve your memory and strengthen your problem-solving skills.

Break the ice with a magic trick that you've learned and mastered as a 30-day challenge at the next social gathering.

Know how to perform a party trick can also enhance your memory and improve your problem-solving abilities as well as inspiring and impressing your friends.

Be more generous and charitable

Try to be more generous for the next 30 days if you want to boost the overall quality of life. It has been proven that kindness makes us happier.

Generous and benevolent people are healthier than their non-generous, stingy counterparts, and they tend to live longer.

Tend to a plant

Try to raise a plant for a month if you're looking for a fun 30-day challenge concept. If you are not a green thumb, selecting low-maintenance indoor plants like a sansevieria or a chlorophyte (ask them from your local nursery or botanical garden) will be the way to succeed in this challenge.

While helping to improve indoor air quality, plants also help people recover, be conscious, and be happier.

Record your dreams in a dream journal

Having a dream newspaper is one way to keep a document of your dreams, just in case you get a brilliant idea while dreaming. More significantly, a dream newspaper is one of the best ways to help you understand yourself, helping you to become self-conscious.

Write letters to yourself

Imagine the joy of reading letters that you wrote to yourself a few months ago. This exercise improves your sense of gratitude for your life and is a wonderful souvenir of your self-discovery journey.

So, what are you thinking about? You can give advice about something to your future self, tell yourself about the three most influential & amazing people in your life and why, and write about things you're looking forward to.

Give yourself compliments

According to therapist Joy Harden Bradford, positive self-talk helps to bring your mind to the good things in your life. So, be aware of your thoughts throughout the month, especially when you are under pressure.

Indicate and correct the negative thoughts you have about yourself and replace them with statements or words of encouragement.

Subscribe to a newsletter service

Read what they're sending you!

It's a fantastic newsletter. They provide you with information on topics of interest and keep you up-to-date on the latest in your industry.

Stop swearing

Swearing is widely regarded as a bad personal practice. For many people, it's disrespectful, and it can deter you from being the best version of you.

Learn to play a musical instrument

Evidence shows that playing a musical instrument will enhance your memory. That's just one of the reasons for making this a 30day challenge.

Other big benefits of learning how to play instruments like guitar, piano, or saxophone include increased self-confidence, a developed sense of discipline, and less stress.

Read 20 pages a day

Writing 20 pages a day 30 days a day is 600 words — nearly three books on average! To read these 20 pages, you can set aside a few minutes or an hour each day.

Write one poem daily

By writing a poem every day, you can improve your writing skills. You will develop a richer vocabulary through this exercise and continue focusing on metaphors.

You can also reap some personal benefits for 30 days from writing poems. It's a form of therapy that allows you to express your emotions. You may develop empathy for others, as well as a new and deeper view of life and the whole world.

Create a personal blog

These days, as a lucrative venture, many people look at blogging. As blogging started, however, people who needed platforms for their opinions (like a glorified newspaper) simply did it.

Some reasons why people put blogs: As a form of self-expression as an opportunity to share a passion As a way of sharing their knowledge Networking Honing their writing skills Gaining more visibility Establishing an online portfolio As a marketing platform If you're writing, you may want to branch out the online and start a personal blog. It is up to you to monetize it or not. Using any of the platforms available today, you can put up your blog, whether for free or with a minimum fee.

Stop complaining

There are several reasons why stopping moaning is necessary. First, you're actually training your brain to gravitate to negativity when you complain too much. Second, being a persistent critic is repelling others.

You are using 30 days to push yourself if you have a habit of moaning and stop doing it. To motivate yourself to stop complaining, you can set up a reward system.

Make a "thirty item personal happiness list" and do one item per day

Although many of us have homes, loving spouses, and fulfilling jobs, we still feel dissatisfied and incomplete.

The way to deal with this is to find out what makes you happy. Make a list of all the stuff. Your challenge is to make 30 days each day one item on your list.

60-70

Smile 10 times or more every day

Even though many people see smiling as an unconscious gesture, you should make it a part of your day conscious. Make it a reason to smile at least ten times a day for the next 30 days.

Innovative lifestyle ideas 30-day self-care challenge pdf feel-good cards 30-day challenge box Smiling will improve your immune system, lift your confidence, and make you look healthier and more desirable.

Smiling has a lot of proven health and well-being benefits. This strengthens the immune system, increases moods, and makes you look healthier and more attractive.

Learn five fun facts about a country from five fun facts.

In the challenge, you will have an awareness of 30 different countries!

Practice writing with your non-dominant hand

You can improve the neural connections of your brain by using the non-dominant hand for tasks that usually require the dominant hand.

Some benefits of using the non-dominant hand include increased imagination, memory improvement, and open-mindedness.

Learn to code

It is a good skill to know how to write code. Just learn how to code, you don't have to be a genius, and you can do that as your next 30-day challenge.

You are going to gain a good understanding of how technology affects our world today by learning how to code. You can also take advantage of your new skills and create websites. And, you can turn it into a full-time career if you find that you have a real knack for coding.

Prepare the next day

We all want to take advantage of serene mornings when we can peacefully prepare for the day ahead, eat a nice lunch, and have time for a quick meditation or exercise.

There are always days, however, when we wake up late and spend our short time rushing to get ready for work or class.

Ease the morning routine by night before planning your outfit for the day. Practice this for 30 days, and you're going to have a good new habit that helps make your morning preparations effortless.

Document whole month by taking a photo

Try to Develop a deeper appreciation for your life by getting your phone or camera out and taking photos of key events throughout the month in your daily routine.

Researchers have found that when taking pictures of the moment, people have a deeper sense of celebrating happy events in their lives. Do this for 30 days!

Stop buying anything new for 30 days

Ready to get wealthier? Buy only the things you need (food and supplies) for the next 30 days.

Create a budget and stick to it

you are looking for new ways to save more money, why not you spend 30 days learning how to conform to your actual spending budget?

Read something relevant to personal finance

Would you like to be financially knowledgeable? Learning something about finance for just five minutes a day will help you gain the information you need.

Avoid buying gourmet coffee

Coffee is one of the few luxuries that we enjoy to make for a hectic day.

Gourmet coffee is pricey, however. Try to make coffee at your own a place and bring a thermos to work for the whole month to save some money and meet the 30Day Challenge.

70-80

Save at least $500 for one month

Save a particular amount of cash each month. Your target is $500 for now.

You may want to stop buying lunches and coffee to reach your goal. Using an app that saves money can also help you keep up with your spending so that you can meet your target amount faster.

Pause your online shopping for 30 days.

With online shopping ease, buying things we don't really need is easy for most of us. So, what if you want to get rid of unnecessary consumerism, make an online one-month shopping break.

A shopping break, apart from saving money, helps you feel more grounded. It teaches you to concentrate on what you already have and to promote an attitude of gratitude.

Keep track of your daily expenditures

Keep track of your daily outlays is a good way to raise financial consciousness. It is a positive step in the direction of good financial management.

Use a small notebook to write down all the expenses you have up to the last penny throughout the day. Read what you wrote in the journal at the end of the month. By then, you'll be more conscious of your spending habits, places where you tend to spend too much, and ways to save money.

Bring a packed lunch to work

The average workplace cost of lunch is $11. But when you cook lunch at home and bring it to work, it usually costs just half as much. In fact, packed lunches are often safer because you know exactly what's in them.

Pay for your purchases only in cash

When you use your cards to make purchases, we prefer to overpay. If you are facing this challenge, pay for your transactions (except bills and mortgages) for the next 30 days only in cash.

Because when you pay cash, your purchasing power is more restricted, you will find that you are becoming more aware of the things you purchase.

Start a business on the side

Do you have any background in small appliances repairing? Are you good at the craft? Can you write articles about the murderer? Choose something you love doing and make money out of it.

In your neighborhood or online, you can offer your services.

Set up a money jar

Put all of your cash change in a jar for a month at the end of each day, then count how much you have at the end of the 30-day challenge.

Learn about investments

You will learn the basics of investing if you are serious about achieving your financial goals. So, when the time comes, and you get interested in investing your hard-earned money, you will make the best decisions about the investments you make.

For couples, how to build a 30-day challenge. Learn the basics of investing in your financial goals are to be achieved.

One way to acquire the skills you need is to enroll in online investment courses.

Get the right amount of sleep

By getting the right amount of sleep, you will enjoy a whole range of benefits. Make a point to be in bed before midnight for the next 30 nights and record at least seven hours.

Quit consuming sugar

Are you sugar addicted? There are a lot of people. Use this challenge to reduce your sugar consumption seriously.

Sugar has been diagnosed as one of the unhealthiest things we eat every day. Imagine how you can improve your health by eliminating sugar from your diet.

Avoid social media for a month

Despite the benefits of using social media, its negative effects still outweigh the positive ones. For a month, wean yourself from Facebook, Instagram, and Twitter, and see how your quality of life has improved.

Start doing yoga

You need to do something to fill the void if you commit to giving up social media for a month. How about a month's yoga trial?

Add up the health benefits. You're going to wake up feeling better, and you're going to be mentally alert, calmer, and more flexible.

Brush your teeth daily

Dentist recommends us that we should brush our teeth at least two times a day. Many men, though, are tempted to brush once after a long day at work or a party night. Make it a habit for an entire month to brush your teeth twice a day to maintain good oral health.

Take your daily supplements

Your health is important, and when there are others who count on you, it becomes even more important. Eating and consuming the right kinds of food are effective ways to stay well. Another way to do this is to take nutritional supplements. Not miss a day to take your daily vitamins as a reward. Your body is going to thank you for that.

Walk or bike

Instead of driving or using a car, a bicycle, or a walk to work, or when you are on a near-home errand. Your wellbeing will benefit from the exercise, you will save money that you would otherwise use for gas or travel, and it is good for the environment.

Eat breakfast.

The importance of eating breakfast cannot be emphasized. Try to make it a reason to have breakfast shortly after waking up for the next 30 days.

Eating breakfast is very important. Daily habit challenge 30-day junk food challenge 30-day list challenge. Be sure to eat when you wake up soon.

Vegetables & fruits are necessary for a good diet. Eating at least one vegetable containing meal a day can reduce chronic disease risk significantly.

Find out some balanced slow cooker recipes for ideas on what to prepare this week.

Train your taste buds

Many of us are choosy eaters to some degree. How about an introduction to several new dishes for a month? Take this opportunity as a gastronomic and gustative adventure. You can go to exotic restaurants or have your own meals prepared.

Increase your water intake

Every day, many of us need to drink more water than we eat. Challenge yourself to increase your water intake. I guarantee that after a few days of growing your hydration levels, you will notice a massive difference in your energy, mood, and resistance to disease.

Lessen your screen time

Many of us started watching television when we were still children. Parents used the monitor to make things happen around the home as a babysitter replacement. It is difficult to kick this habit now that we're adults.

Much adverse health and social consequences have been linked to excessive television watching.

90-100

No screen time an hour before bedtime

Sleep better by one hour before bedtime before midnight, adopting a no-screen-time rule. You may pursue this as a personal challenge or make it a joint objective by involving the whole household (children and spouse) for this 30DC.

Log all the food

This would change your life positively if you track all the food you eat. Not only does nutrition monitoring help you keep track of food types that cause you to lose weight or gain weight, but it can also identify food intolerances and factors that cause you to eat unhealthily.

Try to make a one-month food log and see where a better health journey can take you.

Do some brain-flexing exercises

When we grow older, and our memory begins to fail, our brains lose plasticity. By involving the brain every day in specific activities, such results can be slowed down.

Cooking without looking at the recipe by taking handwritten notes Taking another route from work on the way home Playing some fast, online games involving solving.

Get up earlier

One typical pattern for the most successful people. They seem to wake up earlier than the rest of us.

Make it a habit to stand up as a challenge to yourself at least 15 minutes earlier than usual.

Have a healthy smoothie for breakfast

Earlier, we found that eating breakfast is essential for staying healthy. How about the starting habit of having a healthy smoothie breakfast for the next 30 days?

Eat fresh fruits every day

Fruits will fill the nutritional holes in your diet, particularly about vitamins and minerals that are under-consumed. You also reduce your risk of developing heart disease when you eat fruit daily. In fact, fruits encourage healthy digestion.

Take an afternoon nap

It's an understatement to say that naps are right for you. Generally, you are more alert after a rest, enhancing your efficiency in the task at hand. It also helps to prevent accidents and errors.

Most people can benefit from a nap's rejuvenating effects in our sleep-deprived society. So why not challenge yourself every day for a whole month to take an afternoon siesta?

Aim to walk 10,000 daily

Improve your health dramatically within 30 days (live longer, be at your ideal weight, improve your mental abilities) by encouraging you to walk 10,000 steps a day. Use an accurate pedometer to get a precise count of steps.

Stop eating fast food

Because of its ease and addictive flavors, most of us are drawn to fast food. Our nutrition, however, suffers from the ingestion of too many fries, soft drinks, and burgers of double cheese.

Improve your meals ' nutritional value by avoiding a month's fast food. Replace these low-nutrient meals with whole, home-cooked food.

Stop a vice

Whether it's cigarettes, drinking alcohol, or watching porn, continue your commitment by making it a 30DC to stop a bad habit. Having completed the challenge, you will most definitely have a greater resolve to leave for good.

Practice thinking positive thoughts.

People who tend to think positively can cope with stress better. You also tend to be happier and more successful in life.

Seek a daily dose of positiveness to encourage success and happiness in your life. Maybe you'd like to visit this post for 29 experience and work positivity tips.

Drink only water

30-day nutrition challenge list innovative 30-day challenges 30-day fun challenge Drinking water has many advantages, including weight loss, increased alertness, and stronger bones.

Drink just 30 days of water and reap these probable benefits: Strengthened heart youth appearance Enhanced alertness weight loss Strong bones, Improved metabolism, Stronger immunity Better digestion. Try to do daily bases oil pulling. Oil pulling is one of age-old practice where you swallow natural oil to get rid of bacteria in your mouth. Healthy teeth and gums are said to be encouraged.

Try pulling oil for 30 days to improve oral health. Just weigh a tablespoon of coconut or olive oil, then suck it in your mouth for 10-15 minutes. Do not swallow any of them. You should spit in the garbage after the allotted time. Never spit in the sink or tank of the toilet.

Eliminate single-use plastic containers

Reusing containers reduces the amount of waste that goes to landfills. Choose to hold water bottles of stainless steel rather than plastic ones. Carry a cloth bag or some BPA-free plastic containers to your purchases on your next shopping trip.

Grow an herb and vegetable garden

You are self-sufficient in backyard gardening. It may also help eliminate food waste and reduces the impact on the environment compared to products from industrialized farms using pesticide & fertilizers that are leached into the soil. With this, there's no beating the sense of pride you get when you feed yourself fruits and vegetables.

Minimize the amount of waste

In plus to using reusable containers, you can also reduce your waste volume by learning to repair things instead of discarding them, learning to compost, and canceling unnecessary subscriptions to get rid of junk mail.

Buy local produce

First, you're assured that what you're buying is fresh and in season. Second, you are also assured to be free of toxic chemicals that you are eating. Therefore, you interact with the other members of your family when you buy local. Last but not least, your local business support ensures that the money stays in the community rather than being drunk into a chain store.

Start composting

Composting is one way to reduce every week the amount of garbage you throw away. If you have a garden, you can use the compost's nutrient-rich soil as a fertilizer to eliminate the need for toxic pesticides. You're going to be healthier and at the same time do something good for the planet.

If you join this challenge by using eco-friendly goods and doing things that reduce your carbon footprint, such as some of those listed above, you commit to 30 days of sustainable living.

Challenges for the Home

12 Week Challenges. Donate one object every day from your home.

Choose an item from your house every day that you don't need anymore, but it can still be useful to someone else. Donate this item to the goodwill closest to you. If you donate them to orphanages or clinics, old toys can have new owners.

Organize area in your home

By organizing one area of your house each day, create a relaxed, clean, and safe environment. Choose a specific area to be cleaned up for each day of your 30DC. Get rid of clutter, but useful objects, clean, and wipe the windows and walls down.

You may have set up a solid declutter habit by the end of the challenge.

Feng shui

Feng shui method is a system that considers the harmony of elements in a building to maximize beneficial effects for the occupants of the building.

Try to arrange your home to attract positivity and wealth 5 in accordance with feng shui tips.

Chapter 5: Be Realistic in your Life

5.1 Make Better Choices Easier

We know that making healthy choices will help us to feel better and live longer. You may already have tried eating better, getting more exercise or sleeping, quitting smoking, or reducing stress. It's not that easy. But research shows how your ability to create and maintain a healthy lifestyle can be enhanced.

It's frustrating when you're trying to make healthy changes and reach a goal to experience setbacks. The better news is that decades of research show that change is possible, and there are proven strategies that you can use to set yourself up for success. Many things that you do have an impact on your health and quality of life, now and in the future. Through making healthy choices, you can reduce your risk to the most serious, costly, and preventable health issues — such as heart disease, stroke, cancer, type 2 diabetes, and obesity.

5.2 Know Your Habits

The first step toward change is your behavior is to raise awareness of what you are doing on a regular basis. Dr. Lisa, a Dartmouth College behavior change expert. "try to Look for those patterns in your own behavior and what is triggering unhealthy habit you want to change." You may eat too much while watching TV or join a smoke break friend even if you don't want a cigarette. "You can develop ways to disrupt and create new patterns. Eat meals off with the TV, for example, or join friends for healthy activities, such as walk breaks.

5.3 Make Plans

Make plans that include small, reasonable goals and specific actions that you are going to take to reach them.

"If you walk through the vending machine at work every afternoon and buy junk food, try walking a different way to reduce that decision and bring healthy snacks from home, "Make the healthy choice the easy choice whenever possible." Consider what you think you need to succeed. To achieve your goals, how can you change things around you? You may need to store healthy foods, get rid of temptations, or find a special place to relax.

Stay acquainted with friends and loved ones. Research shows that healthy habits of individuals appear to mimic those of their family and friends. Invite them to join you and help you stay on board.

Planning for barriers is also necessary. Think about what your best efforts to live healthier might derail. In unexpected situations, in stressful times, or when tempted by old habits, how can you still make healthy choices?

5.4 Stay on Track

You can feel exciting and rewarding to do positive things for yourself. But when you wonder if you can stick with it, there will be times as well.

"Identify and turn negative thoughts into realistic, productive thoughts," advises.

It can help to keep a record. To note different things like your diet, exercise, stress levels, or sleep patterns, you can use a paper journal or computer program or mobile app. A study of different people who lost at least 30 pounds and held their weight off for at least one year showed that they often closely monitored their progress.

"Even if you think you're going to' fall off the car,' keep going. Keep tracking your behavior. Sometimes when you feel like you're struggling, you will learn the most. "In a moment of weakness, and others are focusing on digital technologies, such as mobile apps. Her group also uses technology to learn more about how our actions can be assessed and increased.

"More we practice self-control, the better we become at it," says Dr. Leonard Epstein, who at the University of Buffalo is researching behavioral change and decision making. "You are developing the ability to act and react differently

5.5 Think About the Future

Epstein found that some people have a harder time to resist their impulses than others. He calls this "delay discount," where you are discounting, or undervaluing, the larger benefits of waiting for smaller immediate rewards. This can lead to too much food, substance abuse, smoking or shopping, or risky sexual behavior.

"By episodic future thinking, you will learn to delay immediate gratification, or to envision vividly possible positive experiences or incentives," he says. "It's a smart way to enhance the decision-making ability that's safer for you in the long run." Epstein is now researching how to use this technique to help people at risk of type 2 diabetes prevent disease.

Focusing on how a shift will help your body heal and improve your life. You drop your risk of a heart attack within 24 hours when you stop smoking. Stress reduction will lead to better relationships. Even small improvements in nutrition and physical activity can reduce risks to your health and prolong your life.

5.6 Be Patient

Sometimes when you try to adopt healthier habits, other health problems may get in the way.

When you really struggle with these habits, ask yourself if there's more going on. For example, mental health conditions, such as depression and anxiety, can be related to unhealthy behaviors. Health-care professionals will work with you to resolve any underlying issues and promote improvement and enable you to be more effective.

You're never too shapeless, too overweight, or too old to make healthy improvements. Try various strategies until you find out what works best for you.

It may not happen as expected, and that's all right. This is a process of change. The most important thing is to continue moving forward.

The microwave's friend

Microwave meals can conjure up images of frozen vegetables and scary-looking meat, but the tool does much more than heat dinners on television. Make a one-minute quiche in a bowl, quinoa cinnamon tea, or even a flaky dinner of salmon. No time-consuming, complicated preparatory work required!

Make three-ingredient meals

Peanut butter and whole-wheat bread jelly are an obvious choice here, but there is a whole world of simple and delicious combinations out there. For example, take some stuffed sweet potatoes, pancakes, and chili. Furthermore, these meals can also be very safe.

Fill up on iron.

Failure to eat enough iron can cause fatigue and depression. Through chowing on oatmeal, lentils, and lean meats keep energy high. Bonus: Iron increases muscle strength, making the workday and the workout much easier to get through.

Turn to soups and stews

Soups are a great way to save money and time, as well as being one of the healthiest comfort foods out there. Try to make a big batch at the beginning of the week, freeze leftovers in Tupperware single-serving, and thaw as needed. And don't worry about getting bored. There are endless possibilities for a balanced soup recipe!

Prep on the weekend

Of course, salads are easy enough to bring together. In reality, it can take a lot of time to chop, cook, and mix. Save the salad agony by loading on veggies, chopping them all and storing them in the refrigerator, pre-cooking protein and grains (we love quinoa), and making a large portion of dressing for use throughout the week. Assembly will take tops of five minutes.

Prepare pre-packaged smoothie bags

Smoothies are a perfect way to fill up with minimal effort on loads of nutrients. To make things easier, add bananas, lettuce, protein powder, and other non-liquid fixations to a Ziploc, all you should do is pour the ingredients into the blender when you're ready to puree. When you make smoothies throughout the week, held in the freezer bags of pre-sliced frozen goods.

Don't hate it. Caffeinate

The amount of conflicting data on whether coffee is good for you is sufficient to make a head spin for anyone. But some facts are not disputed: having a daily dose of java helps rev your metabolism and provides a much-needed boost in energy. Keep French press and ground coffee on your desk to keep your pocket safe, too, so you can power up any time of day

Eat meals instead of snacking all-day

It may feel like there is no time to sit down and enjoy a full meal when you're crazy busy. Rather, it seems easier to grab a handful of trails mix here, a string cheese, a bag of pretzels between meetings, and different other nibbles before calling it a day. While it may not feel like you're eating as much, snickers throughout the day often end up consuming more calories than their counterparts eating meals. Luckily, there's plenty of easy meals to put together and eat quickly.

Eat mindfully

We often end up eating meals in front of our computer screens with deadlines rearing their ugly heads, forgetting to breathe, let alone be aware of how our bodies feel. No matter how stressed, slow down, breathe in between bites, and when you're full, take note. Chances are you are going to end up eating much less (and feeling much better)!

Embrace the Crock-Pot

The only thing you can control with your smartphone is better than a slow cooker. If you don't already have one, it's time now. The multitasking method cooks everything from soups to meats to oatmeal, and all you have to do is only throw in the ingredients and let them do their magic. It is essentially a dream come true of a busy person.

Spice up your life

For all things sriracha, we are not afraid of our passion. But the hot sauce based on chili is more than just torching our taste buds— it also torches metabolism. Instead of adding extra cheese or mayonnaise wraps to eggs, add a spicy flavor. Tip: Mustard is another great alternative to low-calorie condiments.

Let someone else do the legwork

OK, and you still need a little time in the kitchen. But how awesome would it be to deliver your food in perfect portions to you? That's exactly what companies like Blue Apron and Plated do. Although some of the recipes can be a bit complicated, they're very fun to make, and you don't have to search through cookbooks or Pinterest to find new recipes!

Add veggies to...everything

Spinach is a very common addition in smoothies. But what about brownies of sweet potato? Or scrambled eggs from the cauliflower? Whether to bake dessert, beef up morning muffins, or make mac and cheese healthy, sneaking nutrients into otherwise ordinary foods are a delicious (and smart) way to multitask.

Pump up the protein

When hunger strikes badly, and packaged goods are the only things insight, it's easy to choose the less healthy option. But even decadent snacks such as cookies and chips of potato will not keep you full for a long time. By loading on high-protein meals that will fill you up and keep you satisfied for at least a couple of hours, avoid snack urges.

Keep a secret stash of snacks

Changes in schedule and delays are inevitable, meaning that your 30-minute lunch window can sometimes wholly disappear. And while grabbing a slice of pizza is not necessarily a bad option, it's healthier to have an emergency snack supply and make sure you have something on hand at all times. Our favorites: Homemade trail mix, dried fruit that is not sweetened, and picks granola bars.

Say no to bar bites

Wings and beer may sound like what you need after a long day. But stick to one instead of loading on both booze and bar food. If you're heading for a drinking night, eat a small, filling meal in advance to make those French fries less tempting. Fill in a soup or salad if noshing is inevitable and pick one item to splurge on.

Stick to the Original deal

Juice may seem a healthy breakfast option (after all, it's fruit), but varieties bought in-store are normally packed with hidden sugars and have little nutritional value. Some places with juice will also have on hand bananas or apples, so choose one of those places and get your water hydration.

BYO-lunch

It may feel like a time-consuming activity to plan and pack lunch, but it will also help you make healthier choices and save money. Stick to simple dishes such as veggie wraps, quinoa salads, or thoughtful soups that can be made in quantity and enjoyed throughout the week. Any cooking needed in the morning!

Outsmart menus

The most delicious (and sometimes the least healthy) item on the list is easy to say when dining out or ordering in. While we're all about self-treatment, we're all about tactics that help keep track of your nutrition goals. Review the menu online to see what the best options are if you know the restaurant you're dining at. When you order online, pick at least one veggie-based product that comes with a lean protein. Next time you should order the fried chicken.

Try interval training

Busy schedules also mean the exercise is left to the side of the way. But to get a great workout, you don't need more than 20 minutes. Yes, short bursts of exercises of high intensity can be more successful. So instead of hitting the gym tomorrow, get on the treadmill, make some sprints, and enjoy the energy boost after the workout. Bonus: regular exercise is even better for you to sleep.

Desk Exercise

There's simply no time for a workout for a few days. But that doesn't mean that you can't do anything. Although at first, it may sound weird; doing exercises at your desk is a perfect way to sneak your day into fitness. Our favorite movements: curls of the stapler, shrugs of the shoulder, and crunch times.

Rent a gym locker

Although it doesn't take long to pack a gym bag, it's an easy task to get rid of late running. Here's the hitch: it can turn into a month-long gym plateau one morning before you know it. If this sounds familiar, it can be a smart move to rent a gym locker. Despite being a tad expensive, it gets rid of any excuses (and helps prevent back pain from carrying excessively heavy bags).

Squeeze in a quick strength workout.

It can be difficult to wake up for morning workouts. Sometimes it feels so valuable to hit the snooze button. But that can also lead to completely missing exercise, as heading home early at the end of the day is just as easy. (Who wants to fight for a treadmill after school, gym rush hour?) If cutting 45 minutes to an hour in the morning is simply not feasible, do a 15-minute bodyweight workout at home. Another great option is a quick yoga session.

Walk it out

The average job requires the majority of the day sitting in front of a computer. Use that to sit for dinner and drive or take the train to work, and that means your 70 percent of an average working day on your hips. Sneak into some movement by walking, taking the stairs, parking further away from your destination, or taking a trip off the subway before you really need it. Add up all these extra steps!

Turn TV time into fitness time

Hitting the "Next Episode" often feels so much easier when faced with the option to watch next to the episodes of Orange Is the New Black or go for a run. But you don't have to choose either one or the other. If you watch from home, stretch and do exercises of body weight while you enjoy the show. Most gym exercise machines also have fun, so go ahead and binge (that's on TV).

Stick to full-body moves

Consider a routine that targets the entire body rather than just one place if time is of the essence. We love to use kettlebells, play with variations in push-ups and burpees, and jump roping. Swimming is also a great alternative, especially if you are part of cardio.

Variety is key

If you're bored with your workout, it's far less likely that you're going to do it in the gym. By trying different classes in general, keep things interesting. Is your go-to run? Try a class of spinning. Love to hit the room with weight? With Pilates, challenge yourself. Bonus: registering for courses will enable you to be accountable! And luxury studios also sell newbies discounted packages.

Reduce stress stat

Can stress have an insane negative impact on health? Many people neglect to address it. Master super-quick pressure reducers like meditation and sipping on green tea instead of switching to unhealthy outlets. Other easy wins: a smell of lavender, a few quick stretches, or a walk around the block.

Stay hydrated

It can help keep the doctor away with eight glasses of water a day. Getting plenty of H2O also helps you stay full, powered, and focused. Keep water at your desk or set reminders on your phone to help you remember to drink. More incentive: drinking water also helps (or avoids them entirely) to cure hangovers and keeps colds at bay.

Meditate before bed

Days of stress can turn into nights of sleeplessness. And while completing your to-dodo list every day may not be possible, at the end of the day, you can work on mellowing out. Dedicate five minutes to meditation before turning out the lights; it will help you wind down for a better night's sleep, which means tomorrow will be more successful.

Turn off tech

With all that online buzz (Twitter, Facebook, Reddit, to name a few), turning off is difficult even more so thanks to phone and computer pop-up notifications. To help you stay focused, put your phone in a desk, or turn off pop-up notifications at work.

Completely turn off tech at home. Tomorrow will still be Instagram.

Stay organized with to-do lists

It's easy to forget what you need if you don't write them down. Stay on top of it by holding a notepad on hand to write everything down. Thanks to the family. Your boss will do that

Set realistic goals

Whether personal or professional, setting goals is a great way to grow. Make sure they're always true! Instead of trying to lose 10 pounds, start with five. Do you want a promotion? Taking on one task at a time instead of several new responsibilities. Tip: schedule a monthly check-in with your boss, friends, or even yourself to evaluate (and reward!) progress.

Become a productivity hero

Many people are aware of what makes them side-tracked. If you're a time-sucking social media, log in for 30-minute intervals twice a day if you can easily socialize, book time in a meeting room, or go to a coffee shop when you need to be in the area. Identify problem areas and try to find a solution. And don't be afraid to ask if you need any support friends and colleagues are great resources.

Chapter 6: How to get motivated in life Every Day?

There has to be one big question in life that lots of people want to obtain to the base of, and also, it's not regarding deciphering the enigma of life; it's merely precisely how to get motivated.

Inspiration is a funny thing.

As strange as it appears, I do not think that anybody else can give you motivation. Certain people can motivate you as well as direct you in the appropriate instructions, but at the end of the day, you still need to obtain out of bed every morning.

Any various other sorts of motivation can not be received for long. Sure, you may be motivated to get out and ride a bike after reading the life story of Lance Armstrong, but will that same inspiration get you back out on that same bike in 6 months when it's as well cold outside?

I question it. There requires to be something extra.

I most definitely think that we can be influenced by other individuals, and also I spend a considerable part of my life as a health and fitness specialist trying to make that same point, but people need to wish to get inspired by themselves more significant than anything else.

However, I am not there when it is damp and chilly, and also 5 am in the early morning when the alarm goes off. I am not able to give you that press out of bed.

It needs to be something higher than some external pressure. The pressure that needs to inspire you and the strength that you need to win the battle is the battle that takes place between those six inches between your ears.

That's. You need to win the fight of your mind.

We need to be able to remove all negative thoughts from our heads and also not let that little voice win. The sound we need to obtain more powerful and a lot more confident is that positive inner guide.

As soon as you have the right devices to direct you in the appropriate instructions, it makes it all a great deal easier. Just then, will you lastly have the power to get motivated finally?

How Can You Be A Better Thinker?

This depends on how you and your skills feel in yourself. I know I can pass the exam because by studying my notes and memorizing the lessons, I have already done my best. Worrying will only make me dull and forget all those lessons that have been learned. The key here is to stop worrying about things that aren't really important because it'll make just rusty your mind, and you'll lose the self-confidence you need.

Change is difficult especially if you are a pessimist and want to evolve, but all aspects can be changed so keep trying and always aspire to be a successful person eventually, when it comes to work, love life, baking, marriage and company it doesn't matter as long as you enjoy life. Positive thinking can help you a lot to raise your confidence and trust that can be very effective in your encouragement.

Why Would Positive Thinking Empower Me?

There are many approaches to be inspired, but among all those coping strategies, positive thinking is one of my favorites. We can believe in ourselves that we can do the things other people can do, self-confidence is essential in building our motivation, and if we are motivated, then we will have the willingness to continue our work, task, work, or whatever we do. Positive thinking can also offer you a fun and positive feeling, which will help you concentrate on what you're doing. Pessimists have a hard time focusing on something terrible and irrelevant because they always think about it.

Most of us have had the experience of feeling incredibly positive about an activity, an individual, or a result for which we worked hard, but this feeling often doesn't last. The positive attitude is the same as the event becomes a memory. You could know that every morning as a kid, you would wake up feeling great about anything in general, for no cause whatsoever. Think that you can do that for the rest of your life daily. So if we have accidentally learned some patterns of thinking that make us miserable in either a particular circumstance or life in general, how do we change them into a more' thinking-positive' approach?

First of all, there must be three main circumstances: you must be so tired of feeling bad, down, negative, etc. that you decide that you want to change; you must see the problem of feeling negative from a new perspective; you must find or create unique and attractive options.

When you create a positive difference for yourself, you are more inclined than the negative ones to choose the better alternative.

You might start by asking yourself: "Do I want to experience my first day of feeling incredibly positive for no particular reason today or tomorrow?" and "Do I want to feel positive in general or about a particular event or person?" Complete this exercise to make your brain more positive: relax and breathe deeply, and as you relax, letting your imagination go easier and easier. Then picture that person standing in front of you, this is the most beautifully optimistic, feeling suitable for no cause whatsoever, you, you might think-your true positive self. Take some time to feel completely pleased with the way you are; remember how confident you are, laughing, walking, communicating, going. Notice how positivity just radiates from the positive you like shimmering light, notice how the positive you are dealing with problems, and achieve goals. Transform the good around and walk into your true optimistic selves to incorporate it. See-through your positive self's face, listen through your positive self's ears and think how good your emotions are. Spend some time dreaming about how your life will improve as you live as your authentic self becomes more and more positive.

Completing the exercise first thing on a morning before getting up or the last thing at night (do not try the exercise while driving or operating machinery) is beneficial to many people. You can use this exercise as part of your overall development, or if you need an extra shot of that mentality of' thinking good.'

You can not end up anything unless you start. The most significant suggestions are ineffective unless they are logged out. Thinking of something will certainly not obtain it done, you have to rise and start. I understand this may be simpler claimed than done, yet it depends on each of us to get motivated enough to do what needs to be done to achieve our goals. These articles will certainly help you recognize what motivation is, how to obtain it as well as exactly how to maintain it.

How do you obtain encouraged? Inspiration is defined as the psychological attribute that arouses an organism to take activity towards a wanted objective. Motivation is that which gives aim as well as direction to habits.

To get inspired, you should have an objective. Inspiration is an emotional attribute that arouses and microorganisms to take taken towards the desired goal. No goal, no motivation. To put it to get motivated, you must first discover something you intend to complete. Maybe you wish to grow the rare orchid, climb up the most significant mountain or make a couple of added dollars. Whatever it is, you should begin with understanding what you want.

One thing you can be sure of, you will not work just to be functioning, there requires some objective. Now, when you obtain excited concerning ending up being a millionaire, botanist, or whatever, your mind will undoubtedly begin to do its thing. That's the psychology of it. , if you want anything weak enough, your brain kicks in as well as you locate on your thinking regarding just how to accomplish that goal.

Inspiration is the reason for the action taken. It's a child's way of finding the motivation to do what is expected. We still have to have those solutions to get as well as to stay determined to do the things that will undoubtedly bring the outcomes we seek.

The last and also 3rd consideration is that inspiration is that which gives function and even direction to habits. If you assume about, this is rather easy. It is the demand to earn a living that triggers most us to obtain out of bed every day as well as record to work on time. The inspiration is an income, and the inspired behavior is to stand up as well as do what's required to get that pay-off. It the same principle used in various other areas of life. You will undoubtedly be motivated to do what it takes to make it if you desire a degree or a particular accreditation terrible enough.

The concern to be responded to if you lack motivation in any area of your life is this - what do you intend to do? Do you honestly, actually desire it? Is it your wish or somebody else's? The fact is, if you genuinely want anything, you have within you the capacity (the mind) to achieve it!

How Thoughts Can Change Your Life

I hope when I say: the power of positive thinking is incredible, you're going to agree with me.

It seems almost too good to be true to think that your mind can change your world.

Nonetheless, I must tell you that I have seen and seen the benefit that it can offer to focus on the positive.

But let me ask you a question before I get into it.

Can you guess what the happiest and also most effective people believe of the entire day?

The solution is easy. Okay, satisfied people, the majority of the time, think regarding what they want and how to get it. Developing a positive attitude in this manner can transform your entire life.

Positive thinking and self-confidence Start with Goal-Setting. You feel happier and more in control of your life when you think and talk about what you want and how to get it. If you think of something that makes you happy, the brain releases endorphins that offer you a pervasive feeling of well-being.

You grow a positive attitude as a result.

Based on many psychological tests, happy people appear to have an exceptional quality that allows them to live a better life than the average.

Would you guess what it is?

It is the happiness value!

The best news about hope is that it is an attribute that can be taught. That suggests that by taking an optimistic perspective, you can discover how to assume positively.

If you do and say what various other healthy and balanced, satisfied people with favorable attitudes do as well as report by the regulation of domino effect, you will soon really feel similarly, obtain the same results, and also appreciate the same experiences they do.

Happy People See Good In the World. Optimists tend to have different ways to deal with the world that separates them from the norm.

First of all, they keep their minds on what they want and continue to look for opportunities to get it. We are specific on priorities and are assured that, sooner or later, we can reach them.

Third, in every question or challenge, optimists are searching for the better. As they often do, when things go wrong, they say, "That's good!" then set out to find a positive something about the case.

What we recognize is that you will certainly always discover it if you're looking for something helpful or valuable in an individual or situation. And you're going to be a much more positive and also joyful person while you're looking.

How Do You Prepare Your Brain For Positive Thinking?

A simple concept can be used to motivate the mind to think optimistic. The mind's capacity is adequate to dwell on just one idea at a time. All you need to do is keep things focused on elevating emotions before you build the same kinds of neural pathways that are generated once you create a new habit.

When an adverse event happens, note that your answer really decides the result. When such events occur, they often search for a positive response and hopeful lesson.

Positive statements are optimistic expressions that can be used over and over to show you how to get rid of negative thoughts and promote a positive mindset.

I likewise locate inspiring quotes and also messages to be very useful when attempting to cause favorable thoughts.

Decide To Be Content Resolve to see the life glass as half complete as opposed to half vacant from now on. Delighted individuals, rather than sobbing and also stressing about the right stuff they don't have, offer many thanks for the lots of presents of life. Assume that everyone around you has the best intentions. Some people are reasonably good, genuine, and they seek to do their utmost. You'll almost always notice it when you're searching for something positive in their words and actions.

Ultimately, commit to being happy, regardless of what happens.

It's most important to look at the bright side when things go wrong.

Your Positive Attitude In Practice When everything goes according to plan, it's easy to be positive. When you experience unforeseen setbacks and problems, you reveal on your own as well as the globe around you what kind of attitude you actually have.

How to develop a positive attitude can help you in more ways than you might realize. You do not cause your brain (conscious or subconscious) to harbor any negative thoughts or questions when you think about positive thoughts.

You will find unusual changes all around you when you learn how to think positively. Your brain will start operating in a state of free-flowing feel-good hormones called endorphins, making you feel lighter and happier. You will also experience a significant boost in confidence and become more able to take on new tasks and problems that might have been within the comfort zone before.

You will quickly unlock the brakes and witness development as you never dreamed of increasing your self-limiting beliefs. Fundamentally, merely by harnessing the power of positive thinking, you will transform your entire life.

The 3 Habits That Keep You Motivated

One of the biggest reasons why people stop working to accomplish any degree of real success in their lives is a lack of inspiration. Inspiration is what gets you on the track to success, and also keeps you there for as long as you need to reach your objectives.

If that's all the 3% of objective setters did, then they still would not experience the success that they've planned for. And that takes a solid inspiration to place into practice.

Motivation is the DESIRE or the drive that compels someone to START and FINISH every job that they've set out to do. Include a lot more inspiration right into your life, and also, you'll be able to obtain more things DONE, and also as an outcome, you'll experience a higher action of the success that you seek.

If you lack motivation, it could be because the mess, as well as the mess in your room, is placing a drain on your psychological power. Instead of allowing your state of mind to be produced by your area, TAKE CONTROL of your domain to develop the best structure of assuming for your everyday achievement. This will certainly do marvels for your degrees of inspiration.

2. Positivity

Having a positive psychological attitude is a VITAL part of staying and obtaining inspired. During accomplishing ANY real worth having, you're going to encounter challenges and also barriers. You'll get bogged down by these issues as well as ultimately get stuck in a funk if you don't have a favorable outlook on points. By cultivating positive reasoning, you'll be able to see yourself overcoming the obstacles as well as relocating closer to your objective. With a "can do" mindset, you'll be able to stay determined even via the tough durations of your effort.

3. Curiosity

One of the SURE manners ins which you can get encouraged as well as stay inspired is to create a wish for understanding. A curious mind is a mind that is always looking outwards, always pushing the borders past that which is understood. Your brain thrives on discovering new things, so by continually feeding your mind by doing this, you are cultivating a powerful driving pressure in you that is continuously relocating you forward.

Make it your individual goal to expand your understanding every day, as well as you'll seldom be short on inspiration. I motivate you to THINK of exactly how you're likely to use each of these steps to your daily routine, and after that take ACTION on only among these inspirational strategies TODAY. I ensure that as soon as you do, you'll have the ability to access sources of power and drive in you that you didn't know you had.

If you wish to be positive and also bring in success on your terms

Chapter 7: How to Attract Good Things into Your Life Through Positive Thinking

Think positive in your life, and in having this way of thinking, you will find many benefits. You must understand how to do this by using the law of attraction to concentrate your positive energy on inspiring you for your higher success.

As you learn the law of attraction, you will realize that you have a great deal of physical and emotional gain, and as you reflect on your dreams, you will begin to feel good about creating yourself a better life.

When you advance, you will notice that the law of attraction contains a lot of measures and that it can involve a lot of hard work, and if you use the law of attraction, you need to be careful.

Perhaps one of the first moves in the law of attraction is to figure out what you want in life. So you're going to have to think hard about the things you want to get into your life; otherwise, you might end up working hard on something meaningless in the end.

Once you've learned about your ambitions, you'll need to know how to harness the right energy and learn how to turn down the negative energy at this early stage.

Again, there are a few steps you need to take to find your positive energy, but once you've seen it, you need to act as you've already achieved your goals, and you'll find that this also serves as a motivation for your purposes.

As you go through the law of attraction, you can find a lot of opportunities to concentrate your attention on the stuff you need. Don't feel like you need to focus each minute of each day, that's not the case, you just need to direct that positive energy when it's necessary to know how to regulate your mindset.

Don't forget to take some time out and think about the things you're trying to accomplish and what's going on in your life.

To become a good goal-setter, you will need to know how to be self-disciplined while you reach for your objectives and focus on yourself. This will help you identify who you are and support you in your personal and private life by using the law of attraction.

When you have your positive energy, you will find it changing your life, and you will be able to focus this energy on the goals you set yourself, and by eliminating any personal issues you may be carrying you can then turn your power on the things that really matter in your life to make you feel happier and more successful in life.

How To Attract A Positive Life?

A happy life is something almost everyone needs. But they may not be able to get it. The methods are necessary to draw a real-life for you. I'm here to show you a positive lifestyle. The first step in an actual life process is not to give up on your life.

Why is not giving up on your life so important? How does it motivate you to get what you want, never give up on life, and continue to live? These are two significant queries. There are two steps that you must not give up and continue to do so.

Giving up on life means mostly finishing your life.

When you give up on your career, it's going to be over basically. You don't owe yourself a reason to live anymore if you give up on your future. Living life is something you have to work to get through. If you give up on your life, your health, finances, and relationships will suffer. I nearly gave up twice in my life. It's no way to live and struggle to get through life. Since the end of 2007, I have been experiencing many struggles and challenges. If you're one of the long-term unemployed in any country you're in, please realize you're not alone. You weren't the one who created the conditions that contributed to your country's horrible economy. The mix of corrupt Wall Street bankers and inept, greedy politicians who were only involved in them rather than the people they were elected to serve are the factors that led to the 2008 global financial crisis.

This will increase the chance of depression and suicide when you give up on your future. Abandoning life has an impact on every aspect of your life. If you give up, your overall quality of life is going to be very low. If you're going to give something thought energy, give that thought energy to something that's going to help you have that real life. Give thought-energy to thoughts that make you feel good, help you to succeed, and motivate yourself. If this phase has the first critical step to recall, it's because you don't have to give up!

If you don't give up on your life and focus on the living process, then attracting that real life will be more comfortable as long as you don't give up on your life and focus on living life, attracting that real life to you becomes much more comfortable. You give your body and spirit a reason to exist when you focus on living life. Then you can concentrate on living life and make the most of what you have. I recommend you do as much as you can to appreciate the life-life cycle. Meditation is one of the ways you can work on leading this more optimistic and peaceful life. Once your brain is clear from the emotional noise that builds up as a result of everyday stress and anxiety, reflecting on what matters to you is MUCH simpler. One of the things that matter to me is to improve my skills as a writer.

You are on the path to finding the real-life you've always dreamed of as long as you apply the above two measures. Living this is your life. Focus on positive things in your mind and keep going so you can get what you want in your life. Remember that if you are conditioned to think negatively, it takes time to change your entire mental programming. I pray that the most positive kind of life you want will attract you. Good luck!

Chapter 8: How to Gain Confidence and Increase Self-Esteem?

Many of us suffer from a lack of confidence at some point in our lives. A multitude of things can lead to a decline in trust, eventually affecting our self-esteem. Without a strategy, it can be hard to regain confidence and return to a healthy life. Fortunately, the ways to gain trust are not secrets, and in many situations, can be useful. Try these strategies to get them back as life doles stuff that undermines confidence and self-esteem.

Focus on Yourself, Not Negative People Many individuals are quickly criticizing and even insulting people. Ignoring these individuals is the best way to handle them. They're not worth time or energy because they're only going to be undesirable. Kids who are mocked by others must avoid or confront their tormentors with courage or start an unrelated conversation. Adults must use the same strategy because they are usually sufficient, and this will stop them from being mired in the problem, even if not.

They may need to make a statement if the condition does not change. This means that others have to accept us instead of trying to break us to fit in with their frameworks. Just because he or she is unique, no one should feel less like a human. We have to be comfortable with ourselves and communicate this in the way we are carrying ourselves. Others are eventually going to tire of trying to knock them down.

Easy Ways To Develop Confidence

We can start to regain our self-confidence by focusing on ourselves. One way to improve self-esteem is to dress to show the desired image. The thoughts and experiences will proceed as we dress up the part. Practice proper grooming, wear stylish clothes and make accessories when required. New dressing tends to improve the way we carry ourselves, and good posture contributes to this as well. Stand straight, hold your head up, and always make contact with your ears.

People with high self-confidence tend to stroll because they have places to go, tasks to do, and plans to do with others. Walk faster and at group events, place in the front line, showing a desire to be available. When a thought or question arises, speak up to illustrate trust in ideas, enhance the ability of public speaking, and become recognized as a leader.

Focus on gratitude and appreciation. While concentrating on oneself is necessary, it can be counterproductive to put too much focus on objectives. By focusing on shortcomings, it often tricks the brain. They must concentrate on appreciation to avoid it, building a collection of talents, good attitudes, and achievements. It motivates us to be successful in the future. They should also reflect on others outwardly, finding the good in them and thanking them.

Perhaps more than this, we must reflect on other people's needs and how we can contribute positively. Gaining trust from having a perspective makes it easier because it stops us from dwelling on our weaknesses. It also pays off in the form of increased achievement and appreciation to make contributions to society.

How To Build Confidence And Live A Better Life?

Marcus Garvey, the legendary Jamaican reporter, and publicist was quoted as saying, "If you have no self-confidence, you will be lost twice in the game of life." If that sounds like you, you need to know how to gain self-confidence fast. Why? Because being positive is an indication that you understand how to be happy with your life, no matter what challenges you may face in it.

You have a fundamental belief in your quality and willingness to have and utilize skills and knowledge to achieve goals when you are self-confident. You may repel others who may find you too depressing or needy to be around when you're not self-confident. Some of the habits that unconfident individuals display are being too cautious, undermining themselves to an inappropriate degree, accusing situations that are not under their command, thinking in negative terms, avoiding things that please others, or being scared.

If these are some of the challenges, you need to figure out how to tackle low self-confidence and how to dramatically improve self-esteem. Here are three forms for self-help to address this issue and enter a place where your behavior no longer places your life in danger.

Next, to be comfortable, you have to prepare yourself. The most noticeable thing about this is that you first change your exterior appearance to show a positive image for yourself and your environment. At this stage, the way you dress is significant. Always appear well-groomed and be sure that the setting is suitable for your clothes, including being clean and well pressed. Walk with confidence, a good posture, and a high head. Talk, smile, banish, and replace negative thoughts with positive thoughts and words. Through listening to upbeat music, reading encouraging novels, and telling light-hearted anecdotes, make yourself feel better about yourself and everything around you.

Conditioning is one of the best ways to quickly through confidence. You have to note, however, that you're only concerned with signs, and that will only carry you so far. The next thing you have to do is try to connect with what you're most excited about. Many people are struggling with self-confidence because they are banging their heads against the wall, trying to get good at something that is just a weakness. There are things we're not good at, of course, and that's all right. We have all been granted natural talents in the same way, and those who exude self-confidence are typically good at developing those natural talents and using them to excel in all areas of their lives.

Perhaps the most challenging is the third answer to how to boost trust, and it is an expansion of the first two responses. This includes finding the behaviors that lead to your lack of confidence in your life and eliminating them from your existence. Examine how you live your life. Will you rest enough? Is it a positive influence for your family or life partner that supports you in your efforts? Are you eating a balanced diet? Is your job done? Any of these issues can hurt how you think for yourself, so you have to live with them. You make room for motivating behaviors and optimistic factors to take their place by removing bad habits and negative influences from your existence.

You can only boost your faith in yourself. Without you, no one can do it. Start by preparing yourself and recognizing your

118

natural talents and motivations for performance. Go on identifying and removing the bad behaviors and factors in your life. You will soon find yourself loaded with self-worth and self-confidence emotions.

How To Be Self Confident - Tips To Help You Build Your Self Confidence And Self Esteem

Nowadays, ambitions are established a lot greater than probably they were when our moms and dads grew up as well as we are motivated to assume that we can achieve anything if we strive sufficiently. The issue is that often we reach believing that it's feasible to attain things that we have practically no possibility of attaining and also that can be poor for our self-self-confidence and even self-esteem.

One of the most fundamental parts of setting goals for ourselves is to set objectives that are possible if we do not, we'll quit and feel all the disappointment linked with failure.

Self-confidence, as well as self-esteem, are quite affected by our genetics and also the setting that we are brought up in; it's these points that form how we see ourselves and also how we see the globe. Self-confidence, as well as self-esteem, are fundamentally connected, they are two sides of the same coin, yet they are also different. If our self-esteem is right, our confidence is high. Confident people don't necessarily have good self-esteem; that's because some people can create a façade of confidence despite what they feel inside. Self-confidence can be forged; Self-esteem can't.

If we know what to do and how to do it, the good news is that we can change our view of ourselves and our view of the world. Increased self-confidence and also self-esteem won't magically show up, so we have to produce those sensations. Self-confidence originates from moring than happy with our lives and enjoying ourselves.

Exactly how to be confident and boost your self-confidence - 14 Fabulous Tips!

1. Respect how you look

I don't obsess regarding the physical littles yourself that you don't like. However, make sure you take advantage of the bits that you do, such as. Do not merely get crumpled, filthy, droopy garments from the flooring, and say "that'll do." Place some effort into exactly how you present on your own, and after that, you'll feel far better concerning on your own.

2. Consume healthy food

You'll feel well if you eat well. If you eat poorly, you'll feel bloated and slow-moving. If you think well, you'll have more power and also really feel happier and much more lively.

3. Workout

Workout boosts dopamine, which in turn increases energy and favorable state of mind. You'll also look much better as you'll become slimmer as well as extra toned.

4. Believe in your abilities

Focus on what you can do and not just on what you can't. No-one can do everything.

5. Remind yourself of your accomplishments

It's easy to remember the things that didn't go well in our lives, but take the time to remember the things that did go well. Remember the good things in your life that you made happen. Now you can filter that positivity and knowledge that you can earn good things happen, into making some more good things happen!

6. Realize that everyone experiences fear

It's easy to think that you are one of the few unfortunate people that get scared, but let me tell you, everyone gets worried. The confident people get scared more often because they challenge themselves more often; they just don't let fear stop them from meeting the challenges of life head-on.

7. Prepare

If you don't feel confident in a social situation, think about it before you go.

What questions will you ask?

How will you respond if someone compliments you?

What do you want to say about your life, your job, etc. if someone asks you?

When you get there, find out what you have in common with the person you are speaking to and talk about that. Everyone will have more than one thing in familiar with another person, even if it's just basic subjects such as your parents, kids, schools, pets, jobs, etc. Have a few more questions up your sleeve in case any of your first ones meet with a dead-end. Also, prepare a few follow-up questions and comments if you feel you need to.

8. Become an expert

When you become knowledgeable or gain a skill, you gain confidence. The more knowledgeable and the more skilled you are, the more you have to talk about it. You will also increase satisfaction from being able to give help and advice to others.

Knowledge and skills are not GIVEN to some people but not others - they are LEARNABLE, so they are there for the taking.

9. Model someone that you admire.

Think of someone you admire and ask yourself what you like about that person:

What do they have to say?

How do they say it?

How do they dress?

How do they hold themselves?

How do they treat other people?

What is their philosophy of life?

Note some of the characteristics that you admire about them and adopt some of them yourself.

10. Set goals

There's nothing like giving yourself a challenge and achieving it, even if it's something small. A sense of achievement is one of the best things to help with self-esteem. Give yourself something ACHIEVABLE to do, though, or you'll just set yourself up for disappointment, for example; don't give yourself the task of losing 14 pounds in a week or giving yourself just a month to train for a marathon when you've only ever run for the bus!

11. Know your purpose - make sure you know what it is that you want

Don't be directionless. If you don't see what you're doing in life, you don't know what you want and don't know where you want to be; then you're going to be unhappy and pretty dissatisfied. Knowing how to be confident involves feeling confident about your purpose; to have that feeling, you have to understand what your goal is!

12. Don't EXPECT life to be perfect

We have to accept that life will always be a series of downs and ups, and it's like that for a good reason - it's the challenges of life that make us grow and make us wiser.

We can't experience happiness without knowing what sadness feels like. We can't remember what success feels like without the experience of failure and so on.

13. Criticism is not all bad

Don't assume they are trying to undermine you if people criticize you. They may well be trying to help you. Listen to what they say and think about it. Consider if all, or at least some of their comments are fair and discuss what points you agree with and ask them for some input as to how you could do better. If there are things that you genuinely don't agree with, then say so politely and tell them why. Remember, though, none of us are perfect, and we can't expect to know everything; we do often need the help and advice of other people. When they work together, people achieve more.

14. You DO deserve to be happy

People with low self-esteem feel that they don't deserve good things to happen to them. This can sometimes be because the people around them when they were growing up, told them that they were useless and that they 'd never amount to anything. If people said these things to you, then they're the last people that you should be listening to because the only reason why people say these things is because their self-esteem is low, and they need to make themselves feel superior by putting other people down.

You will soon start to feel better about yourself if you start working with these 14 tips. You won't transform 100% overnight, but over time, if you keep working on it, you'll look back, and you'll be both amazed and delighted with your progress!

Chapter 9: Practice and hard work makes a man successful

How long will it take to become an expert in your craft? And what are the people who master their ambitions and do different things from the rest of us?

That's what John Hayes, professor of cognitive psychology at Carnegie Mellon University, wanted to know.

Hayes has been researching in top performers for decades the role of participation, learning, and experience. He's been studying the most famous artists in history, people like Mozart and Picasso, to determine how long it took them to become world-class in their profession. He also looked at the decisions and interactions that led to their success.

Let's think about what Hayes has come up with about world-class artists. In particular, let's talk about how you can use these lessons to achieve your goals and become your best.

6.1 "10 Years of Silence"

He analyzed thousands of music pieces produced from 1685 to 1900. The central question that contributed to his research is, "How long after one is interested in music is one becoming a world-class? "In the end, Hayes collected a list of 500 pieces that were often played by symphonies around the world and considered to be the masterpieces of the field. A total of 76 composers created these 500 popular pieces.

But as Hayes, Ericsson, and other researchers began digging deeper, they found that time was just one part of the equation. Success was not only a product of ten years of practice or ten thousand hours of work. You had to look at how best performers practiced to understand precisely what was needed to maximize your potential and master your craft NBA superstar Kobe Bryant's practice habits provide a perfect example. This is How Kobe Bryant made it to the Top Kobe Bryant is one of the most successful all-time basketball players. Bryant, the recipient of 5 NBA titles and 2 Olympic Gold Medals, has earned over $200 million in net worth throughout his playing career

Bryant was selected as a Team USA member in 2012. During this time, one of Team USA's athletic trainers, a man named Robert, worked with Kobe to prepare for the Olympics. Robert explains his first encounter with Kobe in the story below, previously published on Reddit, and discusses one of the reasons why the superstar has become so popular.

From Robert, Team USA trainer: Before leaving for London, I was invited to Las Vegas to help Team USA with their conditioning. In the past, I had the chance to work with Carmelo Anthony and Dwyane Wade, but that would be my first interaction with Kobe.

I was watching "Casablanca" for the first time the night before the first scrimmage, and it was about 3:30 AM.

A few minutes later, when I heard my mobile ring, I was in bed, slowly fading away. It's been, Kobe. I caught up nervously.

"Oh, uhh, Rob, I hope that I'm not disturbing the right thing? If you are Just wondering if you can help me with some work on conditioning, that's all. I checked my clock. AM 4:15.

"Yeah, I'm going to see you a little bit in the facility." It took me about 20 minutes to get my gear and get out of the hotel. When I arrived at the main practice floor and opened the room, I saw Kobe. It's all yours. If he had just had a bath, he was drenched in sweat. Not even at 5:00 AM.

For the next1 hour and fifteen minutes, we did some conditioning work. Instead, we went into the weight room, where, for the next 45 minutes, he would do a multitude of strength training exercises. Wow, that's it.

At about 11:00 AM, I was supposed to be on the floor again.

I woke up feeling tired, sleepy, and almost every side effect of lack of sleep. (Thank you, Kobe.) I had a bagel and went to the lab.

I recall that the next section very vividly. All the players from Team USA were there. LeBron spoke to Carmelo, and Kevin Durant was trying to explain something to Coach Krzyzewski. Kobe was shooting jumpers alone on the right side of the practice facility.

I went over to him, patting him back and saying, "This morning's good work. Huh? The conditioning, as it were. Good work." "Yeah, good work. Yeah, Rob's thanks. I enjoy it. When did you finish? Get up your shots. How long have you left the facility? OH, right now. I wanted to make about 800. So yeah, just far. "Kobe-Bryant started his conditioning work around 4:30 a.m. for those of you keeping track at home, continued running and sprinting until 6 a.m., raised weights from 6 a.m. to 7 a.m. And finally made 800 jump shots between 7 a.m. and 11 a.m.

Oh yeah, and then it was the training of Team USA.

Of course, Kobe gets his 10,000 hours in, but there's another part of his story that's even more important.

Kobe's Importance of Deliberate Training is not just showing up and doing a lot of practice. He's practicing purposefully.

For training, Kobe had an apparent goal: 800 jump shots. He was dedicated to developing the ability to make baskets. Afterthought, the time he spent doing it was almost one. It sounds simple, but how most of us approach our work every day is very different.

They also use the amount of time they worked as an indicator of how hard they worked when most people talk about working hard. ("I've worked 60 hours this week!") Putting you in a lot of time might make you tired, but just working a lot (even if it's 10,000 hours in your career) isn't enough to make you a top performer. It's not the same as deliberate practice. Most people who think they work hard just develop the ability to be in the gym, not the ability to make baskets.

Consider this quote about the deliberate practice to keep this basketball analogy going "Take into account the activity of 2 basketball players practicing free throws for an hour. Player A shoots 200 practice shots, 50 shoots from Player B. The Player B recovers his own goals, slowly dribbles, and takes numerous breaks to talk to friends. Player A has a colleague after every attempt to retrieve the ball. If the shot is missed, the colleague reports if the miss is short, long, left, or right, and after every 10 minutes of practice, the shooter checks the score. It would hardly be accurate to characterize their practice hour as equal. Assuming this is the type of practice routine and at the beginning, they are equally skilled, which would you predict would be the best shooter after just 100 hours of practice?" — Aubrey Daniels, Each player in the above example, might praise one hour of practice, but only one of them is deliberately practicing.

Researchers noted that top performers were committed to deliberate practice in every industry. The best artists, singers, athletes, CEOs, and business people are not just doing a lot of work. They are working a lot to improve specific skills. For example, the "don't break the chain" strategy of Jerry Seinfeld is all about practicing the ability to write jokes deliberately.

Applying to this Your Life Mozart has been called the "music of genius" and has even worked for ten years before doing successful work. I don't know about you, but this is something I find inspiring.

I don't have Kobe Bryant's natural talent or Mozart's sheer genius, but I'm willing to put in my "10 years of silence." I've only been writing on this page for nine months, but I see this as the start of a 30-year plan for me. And I can win with determination, grit, and unwavering loyalty because I'm in this for good.

You will approach your job, your goals, and your legacy in the same way. You can blow past most people by combining these two ideas. the consistency of "ten years of silence" and the focus of "deliberate practice."

This does not have to look big or impressive daily. And that's nice because it often feels like you're going to fail. Skill development and growth are often what feels like struggle and frustration. The price you need to pay to discover your best work is often what looks like little pay and no recognition. In other words, the foundation of success is often what seems like a failure.

Luckily, only one hour of concentration and diligent daily practice will produce amazing long-run results. And that brings you to the most critical questions of all: are you working in today's ten years of silence? Are you focused on developing your skills deliberately? Or are you merely hoping for the best in "putting in your time?"

Chapter 10: Learn from Failure

Life fails everybody. You're going to suffer from failure at one point or another. If you haven't experienced a few monumental failures before, you'll wait and see. I'm not saying that because my perspective is negative, it's the realist I'm talking about here.

Most people associate complete defeat with failure. I know I've failed many times over. You might have called me a professional failure at one point. I didn't do anything. Marriage. Company. Overall, Life. And I felt a sense of absolute and total defeat.

Yet, I learned some valuable lessons through those losses. I never realized the importance of failure before having to suffer through countless breakdowns, one after another. I never realized, too, how most of the most famous people I've ever lived had failed.

We're learning when we fail. We grow and mature, gaining new insights and perspectives on life, love, company, wealth, relationships, and people. We are forced to establish new links, bridging gaps where we had not previously connected the dots.

 It is part of the natural selection of things here on earth and the great design.

If you're going through failure right now, though, at this moment, you might not find its usefulness. I know the loss wading hurts. The pain may run so deep that you sometimes question your very existence. But at the end of the tunnel, there is indeed light I can guarantee that.

I came away with some valuable lessons during my many defeats, experiences that I wanted to share with you all. I know how difficult it was to get through and loss in the past. And I know that I feel for you, literally, if you're going through it right now because I know how bad it hurts.

Today, some of the most important lessons you could gain in Life are lessons learned through failure. I'd love to hear about it in the comments if failure has changed you for the better. Here's what it's done for me.

10.1 Learn from Failure Phase 1

You should realize it isn't the end of the road

When you fail and fail big, it's like the end of the line. It feels as if all you once hoped for and dreamed of is now entirely out of reach. It will cost you an emotional toll. This gives physical, mental, and spiritual breaks to you.

But the thing is what I realized was that it wasn't the end of the road that failed. Even though it hurt more than I care to explain, I was motivated by failure more than it hindered me. It has helped me build up into who I am today. It's more likely to do that for you.

And while it's 20/20 hindsight, the prospect of failure is second to none. Most of the time, rather than the crash itself, we are more concerned about the fear of failure. What are other people going to think? How I am going to see at my peers? While these are some of the questions that we may ask, failure is certainly not the end of opportunities.

Redefine your priorities

Failure either makes you or destroys you. But until it breaks you, it can't make you. That's the hard part. No one has had a crazy sense of accomplishment without struggling in a big way at first. While some had to endure just a few shortcomings before success, others have suffered from thousands.

But something weird happens when you fail. You start redefining your life priorities. The items that matter to you are rearranged. You look inward, causing your hopes and dreams to be inventoried. And you come to realize the most important things for you.

For most, a crucial step in overcoming failure is this redefinition of priorities. To make room for what's essential, you shuffle things around. When you think that performance is as important to you, then you begin making the necessary changes.

It shapes what you value

Every successive disappointment has reshaped my principles in my Life. They have entirely morphed over time. What I valued ten years ago is no longer the same as today's value. One of the biggest mistakes people make is they try to be productive is that they value the wrong things.

Success can be temporary if you value the wrong things. Giving up is better. But when the principles are in order, instead of being frustrated, you can be able to succeed. So, what exactly do the right things mean to value?

Whenever we focus on taking something out of the world or other people, it's just a moment away from failure. But a seismic tectonic shift happens as our values change to those based on contribution and giving more to the world than we obtain.

It makes you more compassionate

We all know about the strength of the dominant ego. Until we struggle in a big way, your Life is run by the ego. You're more concerned about what people think about you or how much money you spend in front of others. But things change when you fail.

Major failure brings shattering to the ego. You are becoming more caring as a result. With your fellow human beings, you become more in contact. Instead of focusing solely on yourself, it forces you to look deeper at things, learn, and think more about others.

My Life's failures have served me much more than I could ever have imagined. We made me more immature, gentler, and loving and generous than I ever had. I think I would have been doomed to live a much less human life without those mistakes.

It improves your perspective on finance

Any major failure will help you look at money differently. Whether it's marriage, company, relationships, or anything else that you fail. I think I've done that for me. You are forced to improve your outlook on all things related to money.

All our life decisions affect our bottom line. This brings closer the potential for disappointment as we ignore money and treat it with wanton indifference. It only amplifies the odds of failure by adding things like gambling, drugs, and other addictions to the mix.

But I have strengthened my outlook on money through each successive failure. I've learned to respect it and treat it carefully, rather than disregarding it. You have created a stronger platform for eventual success and wealth in the future as long as we can improve through each successive failure.

You're forced to revise your approach

In many of the books I'm writing, I'm talking about the need for a plan to succeed. But it doesn't just create a plan and never change it. Your strategy must be continually updated, calculated, and modified as you go.

I always knew that I was doing something wrong when I failed in the past. I wasn't working on the way properly. I might not have disappointed in such colossal ways if I had planned better. The goals are not supposed to change, but your plan should evolve constantly.

For example, take an aircraft. A flight departs from LAX and heads to JFK. It plans to arrive at a speed, altitude, and direction 5.5 hours later. But what happens if the way is interrupted? Is there any turbulence? Congestion of air traffic? The aircraft is adjusting its plan. It's not changing the objective.

Learn your true friends

I had quickly learned who my true friends were after each successive failure. Most people are doing the same thing. Loss functions, so to say, as a "mate buffer." Everyone wants to be around you when you succeed. But most of those so-called friends will come up and disappear when you fail.

It's feeling painful at the time. It feels like everyone is cheating you. Yet, real friends, not how good you are, love you for who you are. A true friend doesn't care how much money you've got in the bank or the kinds of things you've done.

The friends who usually care about me stuck around. They motivated and encouraged me. They were there not to pull me down, but to lift me. We said good things, not dwelling on the bad. Real friends, no matter what, will be there for you.

Develop new ways

Wild success and failure gyrations will destroy your emotions. Whenever you are not feeling good and reeling from the pain of failure, it's hard to remain focused and committed. Your feelings can be like a rollercoaster ride up and down all over the place.

It was painful for me to fail. It's been emotional. I still felt like I was unable to handle it. Yet, I got off with some essential tools to deal with my emotions. I've learned how to refocus and retrain my mind to see more positive than negative things.

The mind is much like a camera's lens–it'll see anything you're focusing on. It is better to cope with the emotions that could make their way to the surface whenever you train your own mind to focus on the right things.

Look at your faith

Either you believe in God, Allah, Buddha, or just a divine bond that connects us all, Failure makes you look to the higher power. All of us are interconnected beings. There is a metaphysical thread flowing through all of us.

I switched to my higher power because I fell in a big way. You look for inspiration to your higher power, and you realize that whatever issues you face, others have met them before. Whatever faults you have suffered, others have already experienced them.

I had put my total faith in my higher power because I believe there is a reason for all things in life. Loss, like progress, has its objectives. In the face of disappointment, it's what we do that helps to describe and mold us.

You realize that success isn't everything

And say that's almost a crime. But when you struggle, and you do so in a big way, you know that it's not all success. This is particularly true if your values are not aligned with your objectives.

I soon came to realize my success, the way I had defined it, wasn't everything when I failed in business, marriage, and life in general. This forced me to look more deeply into who I am and why I do the things I do.

More importantly, Failure tends to rear its ugly head more frequently when you value success over everything else. But success becomes almost effortless when you value happiness and contribution.

10.2 Learn from Failure Phase 2

You re-envision your goals

I don't think you should change your goals, even if you fail. How lofty your goals might be doesn't matter? What I found by Failure was that I had to re-think my goals, not re-think them. I had to see them in my mind more clearly.

You know how much I appreciate the target set if you have been following my blog for any amount of time. A critical factor in your potential for success is setting goals the right way. I had to go home and reconsider the expectations that I had built in my mind.

You gain more perspective when you re-envision and take a step back. You see things more clearly. You can then push ahead with full steam. You have not failed as long as you don't give up. It was merely a temporary defeat.

You seek out inspiration through others

Failure causes you through others to find inspiration. Whether it is through famous people who failed at first or some other origin, you're starting to look for things to help move you toward your goals. And that's what I've done.

What soon I came to realize was that before succeeding, many people had failed many times. I've been too harsh on myself. And I needed to make the ride more comfortable and enjoy it instead of concentrating and much on the final destination.

If you have struggled, you should also know that in the past, many others have suffered similar, if not worse, failures. Seek, and you'll find the inspiration you're looking for.

You learn to manage your time better

By mistake, I found that I wasn't my time's active leader. But it is through proper management of the time that we can succeed. Because we all have the same amount of time in the world, I knew I had to make some changes and quickly.

Since no one has more time than the other, in life, it is the great equalizer. While all else may be different, we have the same amount of time. What I came to understand soon that everything that mattered was what I wanted to do with that time, not how much I felt I had.

I defaulted to manage the quadrant time system. I started with the first two weeks of auditing my time. All I did was classified and put in one of the four quadrants based on urgency and significance. Then I analyzed the results and followed the process until it became a habit.

Figure out ways to plan your day

I've never been prominent in the proverbial day's to-dodo lists. I kept the things in my head. That's how I thought it was more straightforward. What I did not realize at that time was just how distracted and off-tangent I was able to go without lists organizing my day. I realized that I needed to create a big plan of action and to set a specific daily goal.

With my lists, I'm not going overboard. I'm just going to explain the things I need to do during the day. I read my long-term goals in the first place. So, I ask myself, "What have I accomplished today? "I think about that as if it was the end of the day. Instead, I compare the results at the actual purpose of the day. Have I achieved my day's goals? Have I adhered to my big plan of action?

So, in more ways than one, I learned to get organized. And I learned to plan my day to keep track of what I wanted to accomplish. It's the little things that count, which you do daily, which will lead to success.

You learn to eat the frog

Mark Twain once said, "If it's your job to eat a frog, it's best to do it in the morning. And if eating two frogs is your job, it's best to eat the biggest one first. "What he meant is that first in the day, you should address your most significant, most impactful activity.

This is also referred to as the day's most important task (MIT). Since struggling several times, what I tried to do was to make sure I was swallowing the froggy. I even tried my best wrote a book called Chasing the Frog, which talks about developing a morning routine of encouragement to help achieve our goals.

At the start of the day, as you tackle the MITs, you build momentum. You also feel more accomplished knowing you've got out of the way the big thing. If you're having trouble procrastinating, feed the snake! In the morning, the mind is most evident, so do it first.

You begin to look at obstacles differently

We're a culture with instant gratification. We want things, and now we want it. In this regard, we are somewhat similar to babies and infants. It is part of our mind's biology as we are born with the I d alone, which is the primal and instinctive portion of the brain functioning on the concept of pleasure. Yet in us as adults, the id-mind is still very prevalent.

But you start realizing that good things don't come overnight when you fail. We can't have and eat our cake as well. To fulfill our dreams and achieve our goals, we have to work hard. I started to realize this more and more when I failed so many times over.

They're fun when the goals are fresh. But the grind becomes much more real when that novelty wears off. We get bored, we get complacent, we get fed up, and we return to our old ways. Our goals are going out of the window. But when you can override this natural tendency, the magic begins to happen. Not overnight, but in due course.

Learn "not to take no as an answer."

After a few major failures of my life, you come to realize what people say they want and what they want. You're learning not to say' no.' No matter what it takes, you keep pushing and prodding.

Colonel Sanders, KFC's founder, was officially rejected 1,009 times before somebody agreed to his chicken concept of the franchise. But he knew, deep inside, that he was superior to his product. He harbored the belief that people would finally start to say yes.

I learned not to answer' no.' I've kept it. I've been consistent. I fall on my head no matter how many times. Regardless of how many times people were laughing at me or talking behind my back.

You become more enthusiastic about your mission

 The first two businesses that crashed are Henry Ford. The first was bankrupt. And the second, after a significant fight, he had to walk away with only the rights to his name. But it was his third attempt to seal the deal. His goal was so passionate that he refused to give up.

I found that becoming more enthusiastic about your goal, the more often you fail is a natural progression. It's the product of refining the ideas in your head, solidifying them in your thought, making them much more concrete and realistic.

You often become so excited that you can taste success. It's not the end of the road if you fell. It's a new start. It's an opportunity to pick you up again and try again, but this time with all the knowledge, insight, and experience you've gained from the last few tries.

You become more passionate about your mission

Failure alone is challenging to go through. We generally make a deeper connection with our community by default. We're going to church, temple, or mosque. To deepen our link with others, we attend spiritual gatherings. We seek mentors ' support, finding others to help us wade through failure torment.

I tried to improve my relationship with people in my community through my failures. I was reaching out. What I was going through, I asked them. And what do you know? I was shocked that they had to provide some input.

Our lives may be unique, but the stories tend to repeat through time. And those tales still occur in the lives of other people. I was totally able to overcome some of my bad and worst mistakes through their practice. And that's how you can.

Develop a sense of community

Failure alone is difficult to go through. We generally make a deeper connection with our community by default. We're going to church, temple, or mosque. To deepen our connection with others, we attend religious gatherings. We seek mentors ' help, seeking others to help us wade through failure torment.

I tried to strengthen my bond with people in my community through my failures. I was reaching out. What I was going through, I told them. And what do you know? I was surprised that they had to offer some insight.

Our lives may be unique, but the stories tend to repeat each time. And those stories also exist in the lives of other people. And I was able to overcome some of my worst failures through their experience completely. And that's how you can.

You recognize your bad habits

You lose part of your ego when you fail. You lose either a big chunk or a small piece of your precious ego, depending on how colossal the loss is. Once the pride is weakened by Failure, you begin to recognize your bad habits.

In your defeat, bad habits get in the way. In fact, in anything, bad habits can ruin all but our chances of success. And I mean that literally. The consequences of bad habits that have been rooted in me for years and years are part of my shortcomings.

But you're starting to identify the bad habits. And you begin to change when success means enough for you. Over time, you gradually change your actions to help get rid of any bad habit that stopped you from succeeding.

You learn never to give up

"I never give up." But, while it seems mundane and over-repeated, it's entirely true. You learn never to give up, no matter what the situation, when you hold deep enough meanings to succeed.

You must keep pushing, no matter how many times people laugh at you, walk all over you, or ignore you. It doesn't matter if only a little bit of change is made every day. We must make some progress at all. We can't stop.

Chapter 11: Pay it forward

Speak to the youth today, and you will find many of them not very optimistic about the future. Feeling hemmed in by the issues of the planet poverty, destruction of the environment, terrorism, they yearn for a reason to hope. Adults, too, are nervous about thinking about tomorrow's light and cheerfulness. We refer to the awful incivility of our times where everybody seems to be obsessed with taking care of Number One on the street, at home, and in the business world. It appears that small acts of courtesy are a thing of the past. In shouting on the Internet, talking in theaters, basic respect for others is not apparent.

This exciting and creative movie is based on Catherine Ryan Hyde's novel of the same name. Mimi Leeder (ER, China Beach, Deep Impact) is directing from Leslie Dixon's screenplay. It's daring to point us in another direction. This shows clearly that goodness and the first placing of others are acts of spiritual beauty. This proclaims that by doing good, every person can make a difference in the world. And for all this, the catalyst is an 11-year-old boy.

In this Values & Visions Guide, the questions and exercises are organized into seven thematic modules. Feel free in any order to use any or all of them. Pay It Forward is a profoundly good film that deserves your most profound attention, thought, and discussions.

Always pay It Forward runs 123 minutes and is rated pg-13 for mature thematic elements, including abuse/recovery of drugs, some sexual situations, language, and brief action.

Stories of Trevor McKinney (Haley Joel Osment) is an older man living in Las Vegas with his working-class wife, Arlene (Helen Hunt), who is an alcoholic recovered. She is working hard to support her son in two jobs, but she feels it's a losing battle. Trevor is a latch-key kid who has to look after himself frequently.

The spirits of this seventh-grader are lifted when his new social studies teacher Eugene Simonet (Kevin Spacey) gives the class of an extra credit assignment on the first day of school: Try to Think of an idea to change our own world and put it into action because action speaks louder than words.

The energetic and idealistic boy has decided that he is going to do many good deeds for three people, something they cannot do for themselves specifically, and then asks each of them to "pay it forward" by making similarly difficult big favors for three others. Trevor starts with helping a homeless man (James Caviezel), an addict to heroin. He gives him a night's lodging, a shower opportunity, and some money so that the fellows can get together and look for a job.

The second mission of Trevor is to bring his mother to the lonely Eugene. The main problem is that both of them have to contend with old tapes of anxiety, self-doubt, and lack of self-esteem. And the physically abusive and intoxicated father of Trevor (Jon Bon Jovi) comes home to make matters worse.

Meanwhile, Chris Chandler (Jay Mohr), a Los Angeles reporter, is knocked for a loop when he is given his Jaguar by a lawyer (Gary Werntz) after seeing that his old Mustang has been totalized. Tracking down the rich man, he discovers that his conduct is part of paying for the kindness he got in a hospital emergency room from an African American (David Ramsey). An alcoholic lady, who lives in her car in a desolate area outside Las Vegas, gave the person a new lease on life.

Finally, Chandler's findings led him to Trevor and his groundbreaking campaign, "pay it forward," which has a very positive impact on the world than he had expected. On his twelfth birthday, the reporter is interviewing with the boy. Soon after, Trevor returns to his excellent work to help his school classmate.

11.1 Service

"It's not a special ability to help out," writes Ram Dass and Paul Gorman in How can I help? "It's not the world of rare people. Well, it is not confined to a single part and time of ourselves. We listen to the call of that loving instinct inside and obey where it leads." What's your first impression of Trevor and his teacher Eugene? What personal qualities do they show in the film that they believe in the benefits of helping and caring?

How would you answer these questions on the first day of school that Eugene presents to his class: what does the world mean to you? How often do you think of things going on outside this city? What do you expect from the world? Is the concept of "interacting with the world" something you were taught as a child, as Eugene describes Trevor's project? In your family, your neighborhood, and your religious community is service emphasized? What barriers have the call of the loving instinct inside you got in the way of your hearing?

11.2 Kindness

A friend of mine," writes Rabbi Rami Shapiro, "is accustomed to dropping a quarter in a parking meter that has expired to save a ticket to the owner of the car. Every once in a while, the owner of the car sees him doing it. The look of shock, he says, both saddens me and makes me happy with this simple act of kindness. I am glad I could help, but I am sad that such acts are so uncommon."

Look back to the last time when someone's act of kindness towards you shocked or irritated you. Were you willing to gracefully accept this act, or was it hard for you to express your gratitude? Discuss how cynicism has tarnished our openness to deeds of selflessness, kindness, and compassion in our culture.

11.3 Transformation

In Heal Thyself, Saki Santorelli writes: "Being broken is the way we unfold. Surely, we avoid this re-framing in a thousand ways. Security is seductive. The desire for the normal, the expected, and the expected soon becomes a trap of our own making. What some of the roadblocks are that Arlene & Eugene were facing as they are trying to draw much closer to each other in an intimate relationship. What of them do you identify most with? Why?

Sometimes it's hard to believe that turning our lives around and doing something new is possible. How would you rate the ability yours to change on a scale from one to five? What significant changes have you made in your life?

11.4 Love In Little Things

The Indian guru Maher Baba observed that "they also serve those who express their love in little things." "A word that gives strength to a broken heart or a smile which brings hope in despair is as much service as a heroic sacrifice. Service is also a look that cleans out resentment from the soul, although there may be no thought of service in it." Those acts of kindness, compassion, and redemption in the movie touched your heart.

11.5 Live With Hope

"Hope is the foundation for taking responsibility, for claiming our ability to create, to make a truly new thing. It is also the springboard for trying to act fairly, and for accepting our incorporation into each other," declares Sara Maitland in A Big Enough God.

One of the main points of this film is that the quality of life on the planet can make a big difference for a single person. What concrete ways did you see on the screen give you hope?

Many of our time's greatest spiritual leaders, including Mother Teresa, Dr. Martin Luther King, Jr., Nelson Mandela, have been an active agent of change and social good in the world. Write some of the moral mentors ' essays. Then think about how to bring faith to your life as an animating team.

11.6 Your Good Work

"Every one of us has a good job to do in life," Flannery O'Connor wrote: "Not only does this good work accomplish something that is needed in the world, it completes something in us. Discuss your response to the end of the film in terms of Flannery O'Connor's comment on good work.

All religious traditions around the world promote the universal principle of empathy, redemption, faith, goodness, devotion, and transformation spiritual practices. What new aspects have this movie come into your head and heart of these practices?

Pay it Forward Gratitude may sound like a pure emotion, but Robert Emmons argues it inspires changes in kindness, connection, and transformative life. And to prove it, he has done the research.

BY ROBERT EMMONS JUNE 1, 2007 Print Bookmark Elizabeth Bartlett is a midwestern university professor of political science. Her irregular heartbeat had become life-threatening when she was 42 years old. Her last hope was a heart transplant, and she was lucky to receive one. She writes in a book chronicling her experience that she was grateful for her new lease on life, but it wasn't enough merely to feel thankful.

In return, I want to do something. Thank you for doing so. To say, thank you. Give stuff. Give your opinions. Give love to others. So, gratitude becomes the present, producing continuous cascade, a process of giving and receiving. Completing and spilling over maybe not to the giver, but to someone else who crosses the road. It's the gift's secure transmission.

Brad Aldridge Real appreciation is what Bartlett represents. As shown by this brief paragraph, satisfaction is more than a good feeling, inspiring as well. Gratitude serves as a critical link between receiving and giving: it moves recipients to share the very good they have received and increased it. Because of so much of human life is about giving, especially, receiving, and repaying, gratitude is a crucial concept for our experiences in society. The well-known sociologist Georg Simmel proclaimed gratitude to be "the spiritual memory of humanity." If every grateful gesture was immediately abolished, he went on to say, and society would collapse.

Yet the advantages of gratitude are rarely discussed these days; indeed, in contemporary American society, the importance of gratitude has been ignored, minimized, or even discounted.

The most crucial part of the problem, I believe, is that because we're out of practice, we lack a sophisticated vocabulary of appreciation. The late philosopher Robert Solomon noted that Americans speak about satisfaction quite infrequently. While being the pillar of social life in many other countries, we typically don't give it much thought in America — with a notable one-day exception, Thanksgiving. On the other hand, anger, resentment, happiness, and romantic love tend to be scrutinized.

Males, in particular, have been argued that they can resist experiencing and expressing gratitude insofar as it implies dependency and indebtedness. A fascinating study in the 1980s showed that American men were less likely to take a positive view of appreciation than German men, and see it as less beneficial and useful than their German counterparts. Gratitude presupposes so many debt and dependency judgments that it's easy to see why so-called self-reliant Americans would feel queasy even talking about it.

We like to believe that we are our creators and that, when we want, our lives are our own. We take things as a matter of course. We assume we are fully accountable for all the good that comes our way. We've won it after all. We're worth it. A scene from The Simpsons illustrates this mentality: Bart Simpson offers the following words when we are asked to say grace at the family dinner table: "Dear God, we paid for all this stuff ourselves, so thank you for nothing." The family of Simpson has earned their income. But he's missing the bigger picture on another level. The thankful person feels that a great deal of goodness exists because of his acts or even through himself. Gratitude means humility— a knowledge that without the efforts of others, so this is why we people could not be who we are or where we are in life. How many members of the family, acquaintances, strangers, and all those who came before us have made our daily lives simpler and our lives freer, more relaxed, and even possible? While it's mind-boggling.

Nonetheless, recent social science research tells us that it will be at our own emotional and psychological cost if we lack appreciation. Researchers have found that gratitude contributes actively to human health, satisfaction, and social connection after years of ignoring recognition, maybe because it appears to be a very pure emotion on the ground, without fascinating complications.

I started studying gratitude for the first time ten years ago. While the feeling seemed to me simplistic at first, I soon discovered that recognition is a profound, complex phenomenon that plays a critical role in human happiness. My research work at the University of Miami with Michael McCullough has resulted in several significant gratitude results. We have discovered scientific evidence that they experience a variety of measurable benefits when people regularly work to cultivate gratitude: psychological, physical, and social. People have reported in some cases that gratitude has resulted in transformative changes in life. Most significantly, the parents, colleagues, spouses, and other people who surround them regularly agree that people who practice appreciation tend to be measurably happier and happier to be there. I concluded that gratitude is one of the few habits that can measurably change the lives of people.

At the beginning of our research, Mike McCullough and I assumed that practicing gratitude regularly should enhance the psychological and social functioning of people; we then based a series of experiments on that assumption.

Mike and I randomly assigned one of three tasks to the participants in our first study. We decided to encourage some people to be grateful and others to be negative and irritable. We also set up a third, neutral group to measure the others. For ten weeks once a week, participants in the study kept a short journal listing five things that had happened over the past week. Either they briefly described five things that they were grateful for in a single sentence ("the condition of gratitude"), or they did the opposite, describing five hassles that displeased them ("the condition of hassles"). The impartial control group was asked to list five incidents or circumstances that had influenced them every week and was not told to highlight the positive or negative aspects of those circumstances.

Examples of gratitude-inducing interactions included "waking up this morning," "the kindness of family," "Thanks for giving me faith," and "the Rolling Stones" to provide a taste of what the participants wrote about. Examples of hassles are: "Very hard to find parking," "messy kitchen nobody will wash," "fast-depleting finances," & "doing a favor for friends who do not like it." Being grateful means allowing oneself to be placed in a recipient's position— to feel indebted, conscious of one's dependence on others, and obliged to reciprocate. An exercise such as ours may remind people they need to repay other people's kindness, and they may resent these duties and even report strong negative feelings to their benefactors.

So, I was pleased that our findings were overwhelmingly positive. At the end of the ten weeks, participants who had maintained a journal of appreciation felt better about their entire lives and were more optimistic about the future than participants in either of the other two groups. To translate it into words, they were 25 percent happier than the other participants, based on the scale we used to measure well-being. Those in the condition of gratitude showed fewer complaints about health and even spent more time exercising than control participants did, and much more time using than those in the state of hassles (nearly 1.5 hours more per week).

That's a huge difference. Participants in the gratitude group have reported less physical illness symptoms than those in either of the other two groups.

We asked participants in a second study to hold newspapers for two weeks every day. Once again, we were shown an amazing form of benefiting by people assigned to express gratitude. We gave all study participants in many surveys, people who kept a gratitude journal reported feeling more cheerful, enthusiastic, involved, attentive, energetic, motivated, determined, and strong than those in trouble. We discussed giving more emotional support or assistance to other people with a personal problem— supporting the idea that gratitude motivates people to do well. And that wasn't just what they said about themselves. We sent surveys to those who knew them well, and those important ones

In Roger's response to that night and his willingness to helping others. As a result, we can notice how gratitude actually serves as "the moral memory of humanity." A second reason that supports the power of gratitude is that gratitude increases one's sense of personal value. We recognize that when we experience gratitude, another person wishes us well, and we feel loved and cared for in turn. If someone has paid a personal cost by helping me out, then how can I fail to believe that I have merit in that person's eye?

This link might explain why thankfulness can be a powerful antidote to a depressing view of life. Thankfulness makes us happier because it forces us to give up a belief that can accompany severe depression — that the world is devoid of goodness, love, and kindness, and is nothing but randomness and cruelty. Through recognizing patterns of benevolence ("I don't think I'm such a loser after all"), the depressed person can change his or her self-perception. We recognize that by feeling grateful, someone, somewhere, is kind to us. And so, we can see that we are not only deserving of kindness, but that goodness actually exists in the world, and life can be worth living.

We are receptive beings, dependent on the support, gifts, and kindness of others. As such, we are called upon to be thankful. When we can give what we have earned in the past to others, life is complete. A 33-year-old woman with spinal muscle atrophy captured this dynamic in one of our studies: all my life, people helped me get dressed, showered, work/school, etc. It was my dream that one day I could do something really important for someone else, as others have always done for me. I met a very lonely and committed man. He and his mother had a boy and died at seven months of age. For ten years, they stayed married, hoping to get another child. They were not able to have a child again. They split, and he became my friend and lover. He told me of the dream in his life of having another child. I became pregnant and got a miscarriage from him. And after that, I got pregnant again and had an ectopic pregnancy. (Thank God, no tube loss!) A shot took care of the problem. For the third time, I was pregnant; our beautiful son was born on 12/20/98. I would have never felt so happy about anything in my life. I was finally willing to give something back to somebody.

Chapter 12: Never Stop Learning

Most people claim to be, and with good reason, "lifetime students." Researchers have warned that if you want to stop cognitive deterioration, you need to keep your brain healthy. But some people seem to learn more easily and quickly than others. Such smart people also demonstrate creativity and innovation, and at their own time, they easily pick up new skills.

It should be easy to learn as we all go through years of training on how to do it. But in addition to basic knowledge acquisition, there is a real art of intensive learning. You need to find the time and energy to build knowledge and skills for deep learning. Very good learners know that making the system as energizing and efficient as possible is the trick. This is how they're doing it.

12.1 Imagine the outcome

For students or people with a lot of time on their hands, studying for the sake of learning is good, but to have intended as a busy accomplishment of your learning needs. Knowing the need will help you decide how much you need to know something and how quickly. Whether learning a new skill set or mastering new knowledge, imagine what you're going to do with it. Get a very clear picture of how it's going to change the way of working and living. Do you take a language class? See you speak to a new customer in a foreign country. New software training? Imagine the dilemma with which you are going to solve it and how it can streamline operations. Successful learners define the target at first and create a strong, emotionally compelling picture of what's going to happen once they reach that goal.

12.2 Think of text as a starting point

In high school and college, many people remember to highlight hundreds of textbooks. And how the words began to blur as there was so much swimming in the brain. If there is a text element in the material you are studying, think of it as just one of many places to store the knowledge. Beginning with the message, the best learners should go on. We create additional experiential learning experiences. We may be sitting and speaking to an expert or thinking about coffee with other students. We watch other people or engage in the practical application of the principles. We know that the book is just one place where the knowledge "lives," and in other contexts, we are searching for it. The more they see the outside world's ideas or talents at work, the more interesting the content is. Then it doesn't seem like a chore to go back to the text.

12.3 Learn in your language

There is a preferred method for each brain to receive information. Some like seeing it sketched out on a whiteboard, others like hearing it out loud, and others want to tinker with it in a practical manner on their feet. Figure your mind's method and translate the material into it. Make charts if you're visual, and find tutorials for YouTube. If you are audible, find recordings of lectures, read them to yourself loudly, and discuss them with someone else. If you are tactile, use it, or create a model, or use a simulation of a computer. Successful learners are very self-conscious of their own learning needs and consciously convey them to others in order to achieve exactly what is required.

12.4 Make failure fun

Only so much can you learn from the beginning of being successful in a task. The real learning comes from testing the boundaries and changing them. Successful learners stretch the boundaries and often fail to understand how things work and, of course, how they don't. You're going to stumble and fall every time you take on something really challenging and unfamiliar. No one likes to look stupid, and you may be reluctant to stretch to avoid embarrassment and ego blow. The more you get frustrated and discouraged, the more you might want to give up. But if in every letdown you're looking for laughter, sharing funny stories with friends and family and laughing it off, you're going to be much more willing to keep trying. Ultimately, it is the act of overcoming such shortcomings that will instill greater long-haul training.

12.5 Make accountability arousing

People work harder when their performance is accountable to others. If an exam is on the horizon, most will study harder. Many practices more if, in two weeks, there is a recital. Successful students are responsible for learning through time and calculation. The challenge is that these expectations frequently fill minds with fear, even if they are inspiring. Take advantage of the nervousness and adrenaline. Create opportunities to showcase your new skills or knowledge in order to drive to the finish line. If this makes you too nervous, make sure your efforts are helped by friends along the way. It will make it much sweeter to celebrate success and learn.

As children, we are born to explore a strange new world. And we dive in headfirst with nothing else to do, devoting all our time to learning how to use our five senses. We seem utterly lost at first, not even knowing that our arms and legs are part of our anatomy. But we're beginning to figure out some things soon enough. We're learning how to recognize faces better than a computer can within a few months. If you think about it, our rate of learning in those early days is really extraordinary.

The world is our classroom as children. First, we learn fundamentals such as sitting in Indian style, keeping a crayon, crossing the street, and sharing. Not to mention learning thousands of words. We grow older and learn about Romeo and Juliet, the Second World War, and photosynthesis. We will look back the year before each year on ourselves and be surprised at how much we have gained. Things get much more specialized in college, but we're still learning as much as we can.

And then we're just going to stop.

42% Never read another book again from all college graduates. Ever. But to make the most of what the world has to offer, continuous training is important. This what separates us from the animals you & there is proof that it plays a role in preventing mental illnesses like Alzheimer's.

12.6 Travel

Surveys show that the U.S. cannot be found on a world map by a fifth of Americans. And some Americans I've heard they don't know where Canada is. If people have such awful geographical knowledge, I have to think they probably haven't traveled much.

Go to a foreign country where you're going to be forced to learn a new culture. And discover that not everyone does things the way you're used to, it's expected to be a surprise, and a culture shock means a learning experience. Even domestic travel can provide new opportunities as you in a different part of the country Try to get used to it in a totally new way of life.

Take up a new hobby

It can open you up to a brand-new world waiting to be discovered. Wine degustation, hiking, golf, painting there are endless possibilities. You're going to learn a different craft's intricacies and meet new people. And these people may be quite different from you, providing you with more opportunities to learn new things.

Read books

You probably have a very close library with your tax dollars that are paid for. You'll be ahead of 42 percent of all college graduates if you just go there and read a book. There's no lack of bookstores, not to mention Amazon, if you prefer to read the latest books and have a little cash. Reading is a cheap entertainment form with virtually no risk of injury, and it boosts your brainpower much more than watching television.

Read the newspaper

Although I'm not a fan of being overwhelmed by the excessively negative news that everyone seems to think is so relevant, you may find some other sections of the newspaper (in print or online). Beyond the news of who was killed last night or how the world is crushing your living standards, there is this frequently ignored section called the Arts section.

Read blogs

Clearly, you're already doing this. On a vast array of niches, there are countless people out there sharing their information, and anyone can find lots of blogs that interest them. Because you can leave comments, blogging provides a level of communication that books cannot suit.

Chapter 13: Never Give Up

Once in a while, we're sitting down and trying to find out what we need to continue doing. We are talking about our past actions and their consequences, where we are now, and what we should do next.

While these are logical steps to be taken, we neglect the fact that adding more things into our own lives means that we need to eliminate other components. We've just got so much time and resources in the day after all. And to make room for what we want to do, we first need to get rid of our bad habits.

10.1 Give up daydreaming

Researched has found one most fantasizing fact about an idealized future lowers energy levels, giving you less incentive to follow those daydreams actively. So, when does it become detrimental to picture the future, and when is it helpful?

Think as fantasizing versus envisioning of the difference between the two. You envision something so far from fact as you fantasize it is difficult or impossible to take action. On the other hand, imagining the future is about seeing concrete possibilities where you can be led by your everyday actions. You know how to step on when you can distinguish between the two, as opposed to pretending to be.

10.2 Give up, looking for a reason to get started.

There's a great time to pursue a target in the trap of thinking. Maybe we're waiting until our careers reached a point, we've accumulated enough money, or somebody gave us permission to do so. And while some conditions are better than others, the stars will not align themselves to create the perfect scenario.

Someone I once knew said there's never a perfect time to start a family because there's always something going in the way. Similarly, you never have a perfect time to start working on your idea, try something new, or pick up a skill. This is the best time to get started. You're going to make mistakes along the way and keep learning.

10.3 Give up waiting for your situation to change

Stuck in a rut will lead to a loop of viciousness. You feel down, and there's nothing you can do to change the condition, which makes you feel even worse. When you reach this cycle, all of your life's components begin to weigh down each other.

Try to focus on one thing that you can work on today if you feel trapped. You have to walk before running. Next, develop a small component of your life.

10.4 Give up doing something just to fit in

You can only pretend sometimes for so long when you're trying to change who you're going to fit in. You get tired after a while. Perhaps you're pursuing a profession that doesn't suit your personality because it's prestigious or because of fear of change remaining in a bad situation.

The longer you spend time and effort, the harder it becomes to cut losses. Be frank to you. To fit in somewhere, if you need to change your preferences, values, and beliefs, it means you're in the wrong place.

10.5 Give up living to please others

Also, you have to take care of the people around you, like your family and the people around you. But that doesn't mean you're going to do anything just to satisfy others.

To your own disappointment, if you always meet the wishes of others, you will end up looking back and feeling frustrated. It's time to pause and assess what you want it to be.

10.6 Give up blaming other people

Sometimes it's really the fault of somebody else that something bad happened. But what are you going to do? Blaming others is a futile exercise that solves nothing.

Rather, it creates more anger and pushes you forward with nothing. If somebody wronged you, let go and move on with those bitter feelings. Excuse me. Reflect instead on your behavior.

10.7 Give up worrying about factors outside your control

Anxiety is particularly prevalent today, with all the incidents taking place in our lives and beyond. Chronic anxiety translates into physical symptoms, such as difficulties with breathing, ulcers, and heart disease. While you can worry about an infinite number of things, there are only a finite number of things that you can control.

Know that what others say or think about you cannot be changed. You can't decide on other people's actions, or how they affect you. However, what is in your hand is to decide what your next step is.

Try to give up fixating on things about own yourself

There are some strange aspects of yourself that you can't change, like where were you born. There is not any question that some of these factors will have a big impact on your life.

But you lose focus on other parts of your life when you get stuck on them, such as your attitude towards others, your actions, and the opportunities before you. Accept the things you can't change, so you can begin to work on what you can change.

Give up dwelling on past mistakes

In our experience, we all have times that could have been done better or worse after reflection. I still wonder if things might have turned out differently if I had made different choices.

Nonetheless, I try not to be stuck in the past. Instead of worrying about what you can't change, use those past mistakes and think proactively about how you're going to do things today. If you are willing to turn them into lessons for the future, mistakes can be used to your advantage.

Give up looking for shortcuts.

Some approaches are more effective than others. For example, it's better to work with a trainer to get into shape than to force yourself to go to the gym. But I don't mean this by "shortcut."

An associate who I know still chases without putting into the work after the biggest business opportunities. That meant not taking the time to earn others ' confidence, losing patience to see results, and making rash decisions without taking the consequences into consideration.

If you're doing an endeavor that took a lot of time, money, and commitment from others, it's not going to be fun and exciting all the time. Don't pursue a magic bullet.

Give up getting distracted

There are always interesting new people, locations, and stuff. Even exciting things eventually or uneventfully lose their luster after repeated exposure. You start looking around and wondering if this new opportunity is better or if you're going to abandon what you've got and tried for something else.

But remember that before you do, it all has its downside. While you may end up in a better situation entirely imaginable, you may also end up finding that things aren't as appealing as they once seemed.

Give up neglecting the present.

Our minds are so busy wandering through all kinds of places that we forget what is before us. We get caught up in our memories, dreams, and aspirations. We are misusing our time in the process and losing out on the moment.

If you're hiking, enjoy nature's greenery and serene sounds. Stop dreaming about your wonderful vacation if you're working on something. Looking back at critical events and realizing that your mind was all that time elsewhere would be tragic.

Give up doing things without a pause

Do you constantly feel that you just have to do something or that you have some kind of plan in place? Although we generally see these as positive attributes, when we don't stop and ask, "Why? "I have found myself taking on a mission in the past without worrying about whether it is the right step to take.

When you find yourself picking up those habits, think in the first place about where they took you and what made you pick them up. Do you do stuff or leap at opportunities because they're right for you, or just because they're convenient.

Give up empty promises

 Things are less manipulative than when someone makes promises but never delivers. Finally, the words of the individual lose their meaning and become devoid of trust.

If you want to support someone, think carefully before deciding to do so about what that means. Ironically, the loudest-speaking people always end up doing the least. You're going to do something this time, take the initiative and help out. Let the results speak on their own.

Give up buying objects

It can be counterintuitive, but spending your money on interactions produces more pleasure than physical objects.

Experiences generate fond memories because of their temporary nature. We are also building strong bonds with the people and places we meet on an overseas trip or an excursion. Yet artifacts lose their initial shine as we become accustomed. So that is why if you want to treat yourself to something, consider purchasing another piece of decoration by entering a school.

Give up taking things for granted

Some things & people we have as a given are easy to accept. Once we lose them, we are oblivious to what we have. When you take things for granted, you can never be happy with anything you have.

To fight this, I've been practicing something here: I say "thank you" to people whenever I can. That means thanking people for providing me with feedback, notifying me of something, or making a kind gesture. The other person feels respected when you thank others, and you become more valued internally, even for the little things. Your surroundings begin to look a little better after a while.

Give up putting aside your health

When you're caught in life's whirlwind, health can end up being pushed aside. You cut back on sleep and miss the workout routine to get more finished. You grab that sugary drink after a tiring morning because you need an energy boost.

Unfortunately, it is not until years later that the effects of bad health habits appear. National Heart & Blood Institute recommends that you measure your cholesterol at least once every five years from age twenty, which means that health is not a "later" issue, but something that needs to be addressed today.

Give up riding the emotional rollercoaster

Don't let you get all these little things. If you've had something wonderful, enjoy it as long as it lasts. If something bad happens, know it's going to pass.

Note that there are finite things, both good and bad. We become used to them even though permanent changes arise and slowly return to our baseline level of happiness. Human beings are people of incredible resilience.

Give up on letting people setting standards for you

You wonder if they're right when people tell you to stop trying so hard. It is much easier to lower the bar for yourself when they show you what's appropriate, rather than increasing it for others.

We find ourselves thinking, "That's so-and-so done, so it must be all right." If there's a disparity between your expectations and someone else's, it's time to spend more time with people bringing you to the point you want to be.

Give up on letting someone else determine your worth

It feels incredibly good when someone praises you. Sadly, the opposite effect of rejection and harsh words is tenfold. When the confidence gets knocked out of you, you instantly feel deflated. Going forward, the commitment to future efforts is influenced by these past memories.

But the fact is, they all have different views. Another person absolutely loves what one person detests. What you are doing and who you are is not going to suit everyone? Decide the value of your own.

Conclusion

All habits of successful people, they are goal-oriented, they are results-oriented, they are action-oriented, they are health-conscious, they are honest. How societies define success, Society, friends, and family can shape your life outlook, bend your priorities, and impact on our habits of success or failure.

What others think can be a pressure-producing external force for good or anxiety. Is it up to you to write your own story? The truth sometimes sits in between.

Performance habits How we define success individually, but when the individual was asked what success meant to them, the metrics were a world apart.

So, most of the achievement on a personal level lies in "being happy" and "being in control of your life." If you add to the mix a society's social perception, dissonance emerges.

This performance matrix refers to two forms of interaction. But for most people, performance at the end of the day is an "inside" task. The conversations We have two kinds of conversations every day. The one we have and the silent internal dialog we have with others.

The silent and often conflicting stance may be the decisive agent for moving forward or still sitting. It depends on what you require between busy tasks to existing in the moments. But it is not in plain sight of the villain.

It whispers in your ear as you postpone a plan or consider starting that undertaking. It laughs in the night's quietness and fills you with terror. Terror is soaring, and doubts are being compounded. Your stupid foe is ever-present.

The biggest enemy, so we often seek out but the biggest enemy? The one on the ground. It's the day-to-day self-fight. That's a problem that we face on many fronts on a daily basis. It's fear of failure, putting off the important things that make a difference, and being judged are just a few.

However, do not blame your parents. Self-mastery is where the magic begins, and performance takes place, and a new battle every day.

Two things are irreversible, the theme that sits beneath and in his creations: life and time. And you can't buy any of them. From birth, they are given to you, and every day, they vanish. Each moment, each moment. The enemy is procrastination.

But I've learned that there are real happiness and success. More things don't equal more satisfaction, but more depression and benefits.

They aim for every day the internal success metrics that include satisfaction, good relationships, feeling fit and healthy, and being in control of your life.